SILVER·BURDETT

Making Music

Resource Book

Teacher's Edition Part Three
Grade 3

PEARSON

Scott
Foresman

Editorial Offices: Glenview, Illinois • Parsippany, New Jersey • New York, New York
Sales Offices: Needham, Massachusetts • Duluth, Georgia • Glenview, Illinois
Coppell, Texas • Sacramento, California • Mesa, Arizona

ISBN: 0-382-36625-5

Copyright © 2005, Pearson Education, Inc.

6 7 8 9 10 V039 09 08 07

Program Authors

Jane Beethoven

Susan Brumfield

Patricia Shehan Campbell

David N. Connors

Robert A. Duke

Judith A. Jellison

Rita Klinger

Rochelle Mann

Hunter C. March

Nan L. McDonald

Marvelene C. Moore

Mary Palmer

Konnie Saliba

Will Schmid

Carol Scott-Kassner

Mary E. Shamrock

Sandra L. Stauffer

Judith Thomas

Jill Trinka

Resource Book Contributing Authors

Jane Beethoven	Activity Masters
Susan Brumfield	Music Reading Worksheets Music Reading Practice
David N. Connors	Orff
Alice-Ann Darrow	Signing
Robert A. Duke	Assessment
Martha F. Hilley	Keyboard
Debbie Burgoon Hines	Pronunciation Practice Guides
Judith A. Jellison	Assessment
Rita Klinger	Music Reading Worksheets Music Reading Practice
Shirley Lacroix	Recorder
Rochelle Mann	Music Reading Worksheets Music Reading Practice
Konnie Saliba	Orff
Julie K. Scott	Orff Recorder
Judith Thomas	Orff
Jill Trinka	Music Reading Worksheets Music Reading Practice
CP Language Institute	Pronunciation Practice Guides

Master Table of Contents

Pronunciation Practice Guides

Recorded Pronunciation Practice tracks are provided in the CD package.

Table of Contents

PRONUNCIATION PRACTICE 1

Au clair de la lune (In the Moonlight)

Traditional Song from France

Phrase
① *Au clair de la lu-ne,*
oh klehr duh la loo-nuh,

② *Mon a-mi Pier-rot,*
moh(n) ah-mee pyehr-roh,

③ *Prê-te-moi ta plu-me,*
preh-tuh-mwah tah plew-muh,

④ *Pour é-crire un mot;*
poor ay-creer uh(n) moh;

⑤ *Ma chan-delle est mor-te*
mah shah(n)-dehl eh mohr-tuh

⑥ *je n'ai plus de feu.*
zhuh neh plew duh few.

⑦ *Ou-vre-moi ta por-te,*
oo-vruh-mwah tah pohr-tuh,

⑧ *Pour l'a-mour de Dieu.*
poor lah-moor duh dyuh.

© PEARSON EDUCATION, INC.

Grade 3, Teacher Edition, page 18

PRONUNCIATION PRACTICE 2

Ambos a dos (Go Two by Two)

Folk Song from Latin America

Refrain

Phrase ① *Am-bos a dos,*
ahm-bohs ah dohs,

② *ma-ta-ri-le, ri-le, ri-le,*
mah-tah-ree-leh, ree-leh, ree-leh,

③ *Am - bos a dos,*
ahm-bohs ah dohs,

④ *ma-ta-ri-le, ri-le, ron.*
mah-tah-ree-leh, ree-leh, rohn.

Verse 1

Phrase ① *Yo ten-go_un cas-ti-llo,*
yoh tehn-gohn kahs-tee-yoh,

② *ma-ta-ri-le, ri-le, ri-le,*
mah-tah-ree-leh, ree-leh, ree-leh,

③ *Yo ten-go_un cas-ti-llo,*
yoh tehn-gohn kahs-tee-yoh,

④ *ma-ta-ri-le, ri-le, ron, pon, pon.*
mah-tah-ree-leh, ree-leh, rohn, pohn, pohn.

Verse 2

Phrase ① *¿Dónde_están las llaves?*
dohn-dehs-thahn lahs yah-vehs?

② *ma-ta-ri-le, ri-le, ri-le,*
mah-tah-ree-leh, ree-leh, ree-leh,

③ *¿Dónde_están las llaves?*
dohn-dehs-thahn lahs yah-vehs?

④ *ma-ta-ri-le, ri-le, ron, pon, pon.*
mah-tah-ree-leh, ree-leh, rohn, pohn, pohn.

La pulga de San José

Folk Song from Latin America
Adapted Spanish Words by José-Luis Orozco

Verse 1

Phrase ① *En la pul-ga de San Jo-sé*
ehn lah pool-gah deh sahn hoh-seh

② *yo com-pré u-na gui-ta-rra,*
yoh kohm-preh oo-nah gee-tah-rrah,

③ *Ta-ra, ta-ra, ta-rra, la gui-ta-rra.*
tah-ra, tah-ra, tah-rra, lah gee-tah-rrah.

Refrain

Phrase ① *Va-ya_u-sted, va-ya_u-sted*
vah-yoo-stehd, vah-yoo-stehd

② *a la pul-ga de San Jo-sé.*
ah lah pool-gah deh sahn hoh-seh.

③ *Va-ya_u-sted, va-ya_u-sted*
vah-yoo-stehd, vah-yoo-stehd

④ *a la pul-ga de San Jo-sé.*
ah lah pool-gah deh sahn hoh-seh.

Verse 2

Phrase ① *En la pulga de San José,*
ehn lah pool-gah deh sahn hoh-seh,

② *yo compré un clarinete,*
yoh kohm-preh oon klah-ree-neh-teh,

③ *nete, nete, nete,_el clarinete,*
neh-teh, neh-teh, neh-tehl clah-ree-neh-teh,

④ *tara, tara, tarra, la guitarra.*
tah-rah, tah-rah, ta-rrah, lah gee-tah-rrah.

Refrain

Grade 3, Teacher Edition, page 40

PRONUNCIATION PRACTICE 3 (CONTINUED)

Verse 3

Phrase ① *En la pulga de San José,*
ehn lah pool-gah deh sahn hoh-seh,

② *yo compré un violín,*
yoh kohm-preh oon vee-oh-leen,

③ *lin, lin, lin, el violín,*
leen, leen, leen, ehl vee-oh-leen,

④ *nete, nete, nete,_el clarinete,*
neh-teh, neh-teh, neh-tehl clah-ree-neh-teh,

⑤ *tara, tara, tarra, la guitarra.*
tah-rah, tah-rah, ta-rrah, lah gee-tah-rrah.

Refrain

Pronunciation Practice 4

Ahora voy a cantarles (Now Hear the Song)

Folk Song from Argentina

Verse 1

Phrase ① *Aho-ra voy a can-tar-les*
ah‿oh-rah voh‿ee ah kahn-tahr-lehs

② *has-ta que‿a-pun-te‿el lu-ce-ro.*
hahs-tah keh‿ah-poon-teh‿ehl loo-seh-roh.

③ *Los car-na-va-les ya vie-nen*
lohs kahr-nah-vah-lehs yah vyeh-nehn

④ *des-de la ci-ma del ce-rro.*
dehs-deh lah see-mah dehl seh-rroh.

Verse 2

Phrase ① *¡To-dos, to-di-tos,‿a-rri-ba!*
toh-dohs, toh-dee-tohs,‿ah-rree-bah!

② *¡El car-na-val ha lle-ga-do!*
ehl kahr-nah-vahl hah djeh-gah-doh!

③ *Do-min-go, lu-nes y mar-tes,*
doh-meen-goh, loo-nehs ee mahr-tehs,

④ *tres dí-as y se a-ca-bó.*
trehs dee‿ahs ee seh ah-kah-boh.

Grade 3, Teacher Edition, page 56

PRONUNCIATION PRACTICE 5

Hej pada pada (Dewdrops)

Lullaby from Slovakia

Phrase
① *Hej pa-da pa-da ro-si č-ka,*
heh pah-dah pah-dah rroh-seech-kah,

② *Spa-ly by mo-je o-čič-ka.*
spah-lee bee moh_ee-yeh oh-cheech-kah.

③ *Spa-ly by mo-je,*
spah-lee bee moh_ee-yeh,

④ *Spa-ly by aj tvo-je,*
spah-lee bee ah_ee tvoh_ee-yeh,

⑤ *Spa-ly by du- ša mo-ja o-bo-je.*
spah-lee bee doo-shah moh_ee-yah oh-boh_ee-yeh.

PRONUNCIATION PRACTICE 6

El gallo pinto (The Painted Rooster)

Spanish Words and Music by Tita Maya

Phrase
① *El ga-llo pin-to no pin-ta,*
ehl gah-yoh peen-toh noh peen-tah,

② *El que pin-ta es el pin-tor;*
ehl keh peen-tah ehs ehl peen-tohr;

③ *Que_al ga-llo pin-to las pin-tas*
kyahl gah-yoh peen-toh lahs peen-tahs

④ *Pin-ta por pin-ta pin-tó.*
peen-tah pohr peen-tah peen-toh.

PRONUNCIATION PRACTICE 7

Hwa yuan li-de young wa wa
(Garden Lullaby)

Music by Chuen-Taur Su
Words by Po-Yang Chou

Phrase ① *Mai mai bay ge young wa wa*
meh‿ee meh‿ee beh‿ee djuh yuhng wah wah

② *jou dau hwa yuan lai kan hwa*
joh dow hwah hyehn lah-ee kahn hwah

③ *wa wa koo le jau ma ma*
wah wah koo luh djow mah mah

④ *shu shan siau niau siau ha ha.*
shoo shahn shee‿ow nee‿ow shee‿ow ha ha.

PRONUNCIATION PRACTICE 8

¡Qué gusto! (What Pleasure)

Hispanic Song of the American Southwest

① *¡Qué gus-to, qué gus-to,*
keh goos-toh, keh goos-toh,

② *qué gus-to me da,*
keh goos-toh meh thhah,

③ *vi-vir en el cam-po*
vee-veer ehn ehl kahm-poh

④ *con tran-qui-li-dad!*
kohn trahn-kee-lee-thhahd!

⑤ *Yo can-to, yo brin-co*
yoh kahn-toh, yoh breen-koh

⑥ *a mi li-ber-tad,*
ah mee lee-behrr-tahd,

⑦ *por-que no hay ti-je-ras*
pohr-keh noh hah‿ee tee-hehr-rahs

⑧ *de la so-cie-dad.*
deh lah soh-syeh-thhahd.

Grade 3, Teacher Edition, pages 102 and 132

PRONUNCIATION PRACTICE 9

Doong gul ge ('Round and Around We Go)

Korean Words and Music by Lee Su In

Phrase ① *Doong gul ge doong gul ge,*
doong gool geh doong gool geh,

② *doong gul ge doong gul ge,*
doong gool geh doong gool geh,

③ *bing gul bing gul dol ah kah miaw*
beeng gool beeng gool dohl ah kah mee‿yaw

④ *chum ul chup shi da.*
choom ool choop shee dah.

⑤ *Son bia kul chi mian sawh,*
sohn byah kool chee myahn sawh,

⑥ *no reh rul pu ru miaw,*
noh reh rool poo roo myaw,

⑦ *la la la la chul kaw up ge*
lah lah lah lah chool kaw oop gee

⑧ *chum chu cha.*
choom choo chah.

⑨ *Ring-a-ring-a-ring a-ring-a-ring-a-ring,*
leeng-ah-leeng-ah-leeng ah-leeng-ah-leeng-ah-leeng,

⑩ *ring-a-ring-a-ring a-ring-a-ring-a-ring.*
leeng-ah-leeng-ah-leeng ah-leeng-ah-leeng-ah-leeng.

⑪ *Son eh son ul chah(p) go*
sohn eh sohn ool chahp goh

⑫ *mo du da hahm ge,*   ⑬ *chul kaw up ge chum ul chup shi da.*
moh doo dah hahm geh,   chool kaw oop geh choom ool choop shee dah.

Grade 3, Teacher Edition, page 134

PRONUNCIATION PRACTICE 10

Kum bachur atzel
(Hear the Rooster Crowing)

Folk Song from Israel

Verse 1

Phrase

① *Kum ba-chur a-tzel*
koom bah-huhr aht-sehl

② *v'tzei la-a-vo-da,*
veh-tseh lah-ah-voh-dah,

③ *Kum ba-chur a-tzel*
koom bah-huhr aht-sehl

④ *v'tzei la-a-vo-da;*
veh-tseh lah-ah-voh-dah;

⑤ *Kum, kum, v'-tzei la-a-vo-da.*
koom, koom, veh-tseh lah-ah-voh-dah.

⑥ *Kum, kum, v'-tzei la-a-vo-da.*
koom, koom, veh-tseh lah-ah-voh-dah.

⑦ *Ku-ku-ri-ku, ku-ku-ri-ku,*
koo-koo-ree-koo, koo-koo-ree-koo,

⑧ *tar-n'-gol ka-ra;*
tahr-nuh-guhl kah-rah;

⑨ *Ku-ku-ri-ku, ku-ku-ri-ku,*
koo-koo-ree-koo, koo-koo-ree-koo,

⑩ *tar-n'-gol ka-ra.*
tahr-nuh-guhl kah-rah.

Grade 3, Teacher Edition, page 138

PRONUNCIATION PRACTICE 11

Erdö, erdö de magos (In the Silent Forest)

Folk Song from Hungary

Verse 1

Phrase

① *Erdö, erdö de ma-gos*
ehrg-doo, ehrg-doo
deh mah-gohsh

② *a te-te-je.*
ah tuh-teh-yuh.

③ *Jaj, de ré-gen*
yah‿ee, deh rree-gehn

④ *le-hul-lot a le-ve-le.*
luh-hool-lahtt uh leh-veh-leh.

⑤ *Jaj, de ré-gen*
yah‿ee, deh rree-gehn

⑥ *le-hul-lot a le-ve-le.*
luh-hool-lahtt uh leh-veh-leh.

⑦ *Ár-va ma-dár pár-ját*
ah-vuh muh-dahrr pahrr-yaht

⑧ *ke re si ben-ne.*
keh reh shee behn-nuh.

Verse 2

Phrase

① *Bu-za ko-zé szállt a da-los*
booh-zoh kuh-zeh sahlt uh
duh-lohsh

② *pa-csir-ta,*
puh-cheerr-tuh,

③ *Mert o-da-fenn*
mehrrt oh-dah-fehn

④ *a sze-me-it ki-sír-ta.*
uh seh-mah-eet keh-sheerr-tuh.

⑤ *Bú-za-vi-rág,*
booh-zah-vee-rahg,

⑥ *bú-za-ka-lász ár-nyá-ban*
booh-zuh-kuh-lahs ahrg-nyah-bahn

⑦ *Rá-gon-dolt a ré-gi,*
rrah-gohn-dohlt ah ree-gee,

⑧ *els ö pár-já-ra.*
ehl shih pahrr-yah-rruh.

PRONUNCIATION PRACTICE 12

Hashkediya (Tu b'Shvat Is Here)

Words by M. Dushman
Music by M. Ravina

Verse 1

Phrase   ① *Hash-ke-di-ya po-ra-hat,*
           hahsh-keh-dee_ah poh-rah-haht,

      ② *V' she-mesh paz zo-ra-hat*
           veh sheh-mehsh pah zoh-rah-haht

      ③ *Tzi-po-rim me-rosh kol gag*
           tzee-poh-reem meh-rahsh kohl gahg

      ④ *M'-vas-rot er bo he-hag;*
           meh-vahs-rroht eht boh heh-hahg;

      ⑤ *Tu b' Shvat hi-gi-a*
           too bih shvaht hee-gee-ah

      ⑥ *Hag ha-i-la-not,*
           hahg hah-ee-lah-noht,

      ⑦ *Tu b' Shvat hi-gi-a Hag ha-i-la-not.*
           too bih shvaht hee-gee-ah hahg hah-ee-lah-noht.

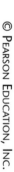

PRONUNCIATION GUIDE 13

Vamos a la mar (Let's Go to the Sea) *Folk Song from Guatemala*

Verse 1

Phrase ① *Va-mos a la mar, tun, tun,*
vah-mohs ah lah mahrr, toon, toon,

② *a co-mer pes-ca-do, tun, tun,*
ah koh-mehr pehs-kah-doh, toon, toon,

③ *bo-ca co-lo-ra-da, tun, tun,*
boh-kah koh-loh-rah-dah, toon, toon,

④ *fri-ti-to y‿a-sa-do, tun, tun.*
free-tee-toh yah-sah-doh, toon, toon.

Verse 2

Phrase ① *Va-mos a la mar, tun, tun,*
vah-mohs ah lah mahrr, toon, toon,

② *a co-mer pes-ca-do, tun, tun,*
ah koh-mehr pehs-kah-doh, toon, toon,

③ *fri-ti-to y‿a-sa-do, tun tun,*
free-tee-toh yah-sah-doh, toon, toon,

④ *en sar-tén de pa-lo, tun, tun.*
en sahr-tayn deh pah-loh, toon, toon.

PRONUNCIATION PRACTICE 14

La paloma blanca
(The White Dove)

Folk Song from the Southwestern United States

Verse

Phrase ① *Yo soy tu pa-lo-ma blan-ca,*
djoh soh_ee too pah-loh-mah blahn-kah,

② *tu_e-res mi pi-chón a-zul,*
too_eh-rehs mee pee-chohn ah-sool,

③ *A-rrí-ma-me tus plu-mi-tas,*
ah-rree-mah-meh toos ploo-mee-tahs,

④ *Pa-ra_ha-cer cu-ru, cu-cu.*
pah-rah_ah-sehr koo-roo, koo-koo.

Refrain

Phrase ① *A la jo-ta, jo-ta que bai-le, bo-ni-to,*
ah lah hoh-tah, hoh-tah keh bah_ee-leh, boh-nee-toh,

② *A la jo-ta, jo-ta que bai-le_él so-li-to,*
ah lah hoh-tah, hoh-tah keh bah_ee-leh_ehl soh-lee-toh,

③ *A la jo-ta, jo-ta y con buen mo-di-to,*
ah lah hoh-tah, hoh-tah ee kohn bwehn moh-dee-toh,

④ *Para_hacer cu-ru, cu-cu.*
pah-rah_ah-sehr koo-roo koo-koo.

Grade 3, Teacher Edition, page 252

PRONUNCIATION PRACTICE 15

Inkpataya

Lakota Courting Song

Phrase ① *Ink-pa-ta-ya na-wa-zin*
eenk-pah-tI-yah nah-wah-seen

③ *ma-ya ma-ya*
mah-yah mah-yah

② *na-ya si-na ci-co-ze*
nah-yah see-nah chee-kah-seh

④ *le-ciya ku wa na.*
leh-syah koo wah nah.

PRONUNCIATION PRACTICE 16

Nani wale na hala (Lovely Hala Trees)

Folk Song from Hawaii

Phrase ① *Na-ni wa-le*
nah-nee vah-leh

⑦ *Ke o-ni*
keh oh-nee

② *na ha-la,*
nah hah-lah,

⑧ *a e-la*
ah eh-lah

③ *E-a, e-a.*
eh-ah, eh-ah.

⑨ *E-a, e-a.*
eh-ah, eh-ah.

④ *O Nau-e*
oh nah‿oo-eh

⑩ *Pi-li ma-i*
pee-lee mah-ee

⑤ *i-ke ka-i,*
ee-keh kah-ee,

⑪ *Ha-e-na*
hah-eh-nah

⑥ *E-a, e-a.*
eh-ah, eh-ah.

⑫ *E-a, e-a.*
eh-ah, eh-ah.

PRONUNCIATION PRACTICE 17

Al tambor (The Drum Song)

Children's Song from Panama

Phrase ① *Al tam-bor, al tam-bor, al tam-bor de la_a-le-grí-a,*
ahl tahm-bohr, ahl tahm-bohr, ahl tahm-bohr deh la_ah-leh-gree-ah,

② *yo quie-ro que tú me lle-ves*
yoh kyeh-roh keh too meh djeh-vehs

③ *al tam-bor de la_a-le-grí-a.*
ahl tahm-bohr deh la_ah-leh-gree-ah.

④ *Ma-rí-a, oh, Ma-rí-a,*
mah-ree-ah, oh, mah-ree-ah,

⑤ *Ma-rí-a, a-mi-ga mí-a,*
mah-ree-ah, ah-mee-gah mee-ah,

⑥ *Yo quie-ro que tú me lle-ves*
yoh kyeh-roh keh too meh djeh-vehs

⑦ *al tam-bor de la_a-le-grí-a.*
ahl tahm-bohr deh la_ah-leh-gree-ah.

Grade 3, Teacher Edition, page 270

Pronunciation Practice 18

Karangatia ra

Maori Song from New Zealand

Phrase ① *Ka-ran-ga-ti-a ra*
kah-rah(n)-gah-tee-ah rah

② *Ka-ran-ga-ti-a ra*
kah-rah(n)-gah-tee-ah rah

③ *Po-whi-ri-ti-a ra*
poh-fee-ree-tee-ah rah

④ *nga i-wi o te mo-tu*
nah ee-wee oh teh moh-too

⑤ *Ki te-nei ma-rae*
kee teh-neh mah-rah‿eh

⑥ *ha-e-re mai*
hah-eh-reh mah‿hee

⑦ *He hui a ro-ha*
heh hoo‿ee ah roh-hah

⑧ *mo kou-tou e te-i-wi*
moh koo-too eh teh ee wee

⑨ *Na-u nei te a-ro-ha*
nah-oo neh teh ah-roh-hah

⑩ *me te ma-mae.*
meh teh mah-mah‿eh.

Pronunciation Practice 19

Sarika keo (Bird Song)

Folk Song from Cambodia

Verse 1

Phrase

① *Sa-ri-ka keo euy*
sah-ree-kah kl‿oh uh‿ee

② *si ey kang kang?*
see eh‿ee kah(ng) kah(ng)?

③ *Ey sa-ri-yaing.*
hah‿ee sah-ree-yuhn(g).

④ *Sa-ri-ka keo euy*
sah-ree-kah kl‿oh uh‿ee

⑤ *si ey kang kang?*
see eh‿ee kah(ng) kah(ng)?

⑥ *Ey sa-ri-yaing.*
hah‿ee sah-ree-yuhn.

⑦ *Si phle dam-bang*
see pleh duhm-bohng

⑧ *pra-choeuk knea leng.*
prah-chuhk nee-eh lehng.

⑨ *Euy keo keo euy,*
uh-ee kl‿oh kl‿oh oh‿uh‿ee,

⑩ *euy keo keo euy.*
uh-ee kl‿oh kl‿oh oh‿uh‿ee.

Verse 2

Phrase

① *Slap vea chakk kbach*
slah vwee‿ah chahk bah‿ee(k)

② *mo-at vea thveu phleng.*
maw-hawt vwee‿ah thvuh flehng.

③ *Ey sa-ri-yaing.*
hah‿ee sah-ree-yuhn(g).

④ *Slap vea chakk kbach*
slah vwee‿ah chahk bah‿ee(k)

⑤ *mo-at vea thveu phleng.*
maw-hawt vwee‿ah thvuh flehng.

⑥ *Ey sa-ri-yaing.*
hah‿ee sah-ree-yuhn(g).

⑦ *Pra-choeuk knea leng*
prah-chuk khnee‿eh lehng

⑧ *leu mek proeuk-sa.*
luh meh proo‿uh(n)-sah.

⑨ *Euy keo keo euy,*
uh-ee kl‿oh kl‿oh oh‿uh‿ee,

⑩ *euy keo keo euy.*
uh-ee kl‿oh kl‿oh oh‿uh‿ee.

PRONUNCIATION PRACTICE 20

Shu ha mo (Frogs)

Folk Song from China

Phrase ① *Yi zhi ha ma*
yee zhee hah mah

② *yi zhang zui*
yee djahng zeh

③ *liang zhi yan jing*
lyahng zhee yehn jeeng

④ *si tiao tui*
suh tyow tweh

⑤ *Pin pong pin pong*
pee(n) paw(n) pee(n) paw(n)

⑥ *tiao xia shui*
tyow shee-ah shweh

⑦ *ya ha ma bu chi shui*
yah hah maw boo shee shweh

⑧ *tai ping nian*
tah_ee peeng nyahn

⑨ *he er mei zi xi*
huh uhr meh dzuh shee

⑩ *shui shang piao.*
shweh shahng pyow.

(*Shu ha mo* = shoo hah moh)

PRONUNCIATION PRACTICE 21

Pust' 'vsegda budet sonse (May the Sun Shine Forever)

Music by A. Ostrovsky
Russian Words by L. Oshanin

Phrase ① *Pust' 'vse-gda bu-det son-se,*
poost syehg-dah boo-dyeht sohln-tsuh,

② *Pust' 'vse-gda bu-det nye-ba,*
poost syehg-dah boo-dyeht nyeh-buh,

③ *Pust' 'vse-gda bu-det ma-ma,*
poost syehg-dah boo-dyeht mah-mah,

④ *Pust' 'vse-gda bu-do ya!*
poost syehg-dah boo-doo yah!

⑤ *Pust' 'vse-gda bu-det son-se,*
poost syehg-dah boo-dyeht sohln-tsuh,

⑥ *Pust' 'vse-gda bu-det nye-ba,*
poost syehg-dah boo-dyeht nyeh-buh,

⑦ *Pust' 'vse-gda bu-det ma-ma,*
poost syehg-dah boo-dyeht mah-mah,

⑧ *Pust' 'vse-gda bu-do ya!*
poost syehg-dah boo-doo yah!

PRONUNCIATION PRACTICE 22

Mübärak (Happy Birthday)

Birthday Song from Iran

Phrase ① *Mü-bä-rak, mù-bä-rak,*
moh-boh-rahk, moh-boh-rahk,

② *ta-val-lu-det mù-bä-rak,*
tah-vahl-loo-deht moh-boh-rahk,

③ *mù-bä-rak, mù-bä-rak,*
moh-boh-rahk, moh-boh-rahk,

④ *ta-val-lu-det mù-bä-rak.*
tah-vahl-loo-deht moh-boh-rahk.

⑤ *La bat shä-di de let khush,*
lah bah shah-duh deh leht koosh,

⑥ *chu gul pur khan-deh bä she*
choh gool poor hahn-deh bah shee

⑦ *be-yä sham hä rä fot kun*
beh-yah shahm hah rah foot kahn

⑧ *ke sad säl zen-deh bä she.*
keh saht sahl zehn-deh bah shee.

PRONUNCIATION PRACTICE 23

Artsa alinu (Come to the Land)

Folk Song from Israel

Phrase

① *Ar-tsa a-li-nu, ar-tsa a-li-nu, ar-tsa a-li-nu.*
ahr-tsah ah-lee-noo, ahr-tsah ah-lee-noo, ahr-tsah ah-lee-noo.

② *Ar-tsa a-li-nu, ar-tsa a-li-nu, ar-tsa a-li-nu.*
ahr-tsah ah-lee-noo, ahr-tsah ah-lee-noo, ahr-tsah ah-lee-noo.

③ *K'var cha-rash-nu v'-gam za-ra-nu.*
kvahr hkhah-rahsh-noo veh-gahm zah-rah-noo.

④ *K'var cha-rash-nu v'-gam za-ra-nu.*
kvahr hkhah-rahsh-noo veh-gahm zah-rah-noo.

⑤ *A-val od lo ka-tsar-nu.*
ah-vahl ohd loh kah-tsahr-noo.

⑥ *A-val od lo ka-tsar-nu.*
ah-vahl ohd loh kah-tsahr-noo.

⑦ *A-val od lo ka-tsar-nu.*
ah-vahl ohd loh kah-tsahr-noo.

⑧ *A-val od lo ka-tsar-nu.*
ah-vahl ohd loh kah-tsahr-noo.

Grade 3, Teacher Edition, page 284

PRONUNCIATION PRACTICE 24

Sansaw akroma

Game Song from Ghana

Phrase

① *San-saw‿a-kro-ma*
sah(n)-sah-kroh-mah i

② *ne na wu‿o ɔ-kye-kye nko-kɔ-mba*
nee neh woh‿aw-cheh(ng)-cheh(ng) koh-kohm-bah

③ *ɔ-seɔ ke yea dwu-ma*
aw seh‿oh kI yeh djoo-mah

④ *ne na wu‿o ɔ-kye-kye nko-kɔ-mba*
nee neh woh‿aw-cheh(ng)-cheh(ng) koh-kohm-bah

⑤ *E kyin e kyin e kyin kyin*
eh chihn eh chihn eh chihn chihn

⑥ *A nan-tew‿a nan-tew‿a nan-tew*
ah nahn-choo‿ah nahn-choo‿ah nahn-choo

⑦ *ɔ-seɔ ke yea dwu-ma*
aw-saw keh yeh djoo-mah

⑧ *ne na wu‿o*
nee neh woh‿aw

⑨ *na je wu‿o*
nee jeh woh‿aw

⑩ *San-saw‿a-kro-ma*
sah(n)-sah-kroh-mah

⑪ *ne na wu‿o ɔ-kye-kye nko-kɔ-mba*
nee neh woh‿aw-cheh(ng)-cheh(ng) koh-kohm-bah

⑫ *ɔ-seɔ ke yea dwu-ma*
aw seh‿oh kI yeh djoo-mah

⑬ *ne na wu‿o ɔ-kye-kye nko-kɔ-mba*
nee neh woh‿aw-cheh(ng)-cheh(ng) koh-kohm-bah

PRONUNCIATION PRACTICE 25

Sierra Morena

Folk Song from Mexico

Phrase ① *De Sie-rra Mo-re-na*
deh see-eh-rrah moh-reh-nah

② *que vien-en ba-jan-do*
keh vee‿ehn-ehn bah-hahn-doh

③ *cua-tro pa-lo-mi-tas*
wah-troh pah-loh-mee-tahs

④ *y‿un vie-jo‿a-rri-an-do.*
ee‿oon vee‿eh-hwahrr-ee-ahn-doh.

Grade 3, Teacher Edition, page 296

PRONUNCIATION PRACTICE 26

La calle ancha (The Wide Street)

Folk Song from Puerto Rico

Verse 1

Phrase ① *La ca-lle an-cha, cha, cha*
la kah-djeh ahn-chah, chah, chah

② *de San Ber-nar-do, do, do*
deh sahn behrr-nahrr-doh, doh, doh

③ *Tie-ne_u-na fuen-te, te, te*
tee_eh-neh oo-nah fwehn-teh, teh, teh

④ *con cua-tro ca-ños, ños, ños.*
kohn kwah-troh kah-nyohs, nyohs, nyohs.

Verse 2

Phrase ① *Los cua-tro ca-ños, ños, ños*
lohs kwah-troh kah-nyohs, nyohs, nyohs

② *dan-a-gua_her-mo-sa, sa, sa*
dahn ah-gwah_ehrr-moh-sah, sah, sah

③ *Pa-ra los ni-ños, ños, ños*
pah-rah lohs nee-nyohs, nyohs, nyohs

④ *de Za-ra-go-za, za, za.*
deh sah-rah-goh-sah, sah, sah.

PRONUNCIATION PRACTICE 27

Jan ken pon

Collected by Mary Shamrock at the Nishi
Hongwanji Temple Dharma School

Phrase   ①   *O-na-ka ga su-i-ta-ra goo goo goo,*
oh-nah-kah gah soo-ee-tah-rah goo goo goo,

  ②   *Ka-mi-no-ke no-bi ta-ra cho-ki cho-ki cho-ki,*
kah-mee-noh-keh noh-bee tah-rah choh-kee choh-kee choh-kee,

  ③   *ho-ko-ri wo ha-ta-i-te pa pa pa,*
hoh-koh-ree woh hah-tah-ee-teh pah pah pah,

  ④   *Jan ken pon de goo cho-ki pa.*
jahn kehn pohn deh goo choh-kee pah.

  ⑤   *Jan ken pon!*
jahn kehn pohn!

Grade 3, Teacher Edition, page 302

PRONUNCIATION PRACTICE 28

Ah, eu entrei na roda (I Came to Try This Game)

Circle Game from Brazil

Phrase   ①   *Ah, eu en-trei na ro-da,*
Ah, eh‿oo ehn-treh‿ee nah hoh-dah,

②   *pa-ra ver co-mo se dan-ça.*
pah-rrah vehr koh-moh seh dahn-sah.

③   *Ah,‿eu en-trei na con-tra dan-ça,*
Ah, eh‿oo ehn-treh‿ee nah kohn-treh dahn-sah,

④   *Ah,‿eu nao sei dan-çar!*
Ah, eh‿oo noh seh-ee dahn-sahr!

⑤   *La' vai uma, la' váo du-ás,*
lah vah‿ee oo‿mah, lah vow doo-ahdzh,

⑥   *la' váo três, pe-la ter-cei-ra,*
lah vow trehs, peh-lah tehr-seh‿ee-rrah,

⑦   *la' se vai o meu a-mor*
lah seh vah‿ee oh meh‿oo ah-mohr

⑧   *de va-por p'ra ca-choi-e-ra!*
jeh vah-pohr prah kah-show-eh-rrah!

PRONUNCIATION PRACTICE 29

Nie chcę cię znác (Don't Want to Know You)

Folk Song from Poland

Phrase ① *Nie chcę cię , nie chcę cię,*
nyeh seh cheh, nyeh seeyeh cheh,

② *nie chcę cię znác.*
nyeh seh cheh znahch.

③ *Chodź do mnie, chodź do mnie,*
hohch doh mnyeh, hohch doh mnyeh,

④ *rąez-kę mi daj.*
rawnch-keh mee dah_ee.

⑤ *Pra-wą mi daj,*
prah-voh mee dah_ee,

⑥ *le-wą mi daj.*
leh-voh mee dah_ee.

⑦ *I juz się na*
ee yoo sheh nah

⑧ *mnie nie gnie-waj.*
mnyeh nyeh gneh-vah_ee.

⑨ *Pra-wą mi daj,*
prah-voh mee dah_ee,

⑩ *le-wą mi daj.*
leh-voh mee dah_ee.

⑪ *I juz się na*
ee yoo sheh nah

⑫ *mnie nie gnie-waj.*
mnyeh nyeh gnyeh-vah_ee.

Grade 3, Teacher Edition, page 314

PRONUNCIATION PRACTICE 30

Greetings

Polish Greetings
Words and Rhythmic Setting by Andrea Schafer

Phrase ① *Cześć!*
chehsht!

② *Dzień do-bry!*
dchihn doh-breh!

③ *Bar-dzo mi-mi-lo.*
bahr-dzoh mee-mee-woh.

④ *Dzię ku-je.*
dchuh(n) koo-yuh.

⑤ *Pro-szę.*
proh-szheh.

⑥ *Prze-pra-szam.*
scheh-pruh-shuhm.

⑦ *Do-bra-noc.*
doh-brah-nohts.

Grade 3, Teacher Edition, page 316

Al citrón

Latino Nonsense Song from California

Phrase

① *Al ci-trón de un fan-dan-go,*
ahl see-trohn deh oon fahn-dahn-goh,

② *San-go, San-go, Sa-ba-ré.*
sahn-goh, sahn-goh, sah-bah-reh.

③ *Sa-ba-ré de la ron-de-lla*
sah-bah-reh deh lah rrohn-deh-yah

④ *Con su tri-ki, tri-ki-trón.*
kohn soo tree-kee, tree-kee-trohn.

PRONUNCIATION PRACTICE 32

Al ánimo

Folk Song from Spain

Verse 1

Phrase ① *Al á-ni-mo, al á-ni-mo,*
ahl ah-nee-moh, ahl ah-nee-moh,

② *la fuen-te se rom-pió.*
ah fwehn-teh seh rohm-pee‿oh.

③ *Al á-ni-mo, al á-ni-mo,*
ahl ah-nee-moh, ahl ah-nee-moh,

④ *man-dad-la‿a componer.*
mahn-dahd-lah‿ah kohm-poh-nehr.

Refrain

Phrase ① *¡Hu- rí, hu- rí, hu- rá!*
oo-ree, oo-ree, oo-rah!

② *La rei-na va‿a pa-sar.*
lah reh-nah bah pah-sahr.

③ *¡Hu- rí, hu- rí, hu- rá!*
oo-ree, oo-ree, oo-rah!

④ *La rei-na va‿a pa-sar.*
lah reh-nah bah pah-sahr.

Verse 2

Phrase ① *Al á-ni-mo, al á-ni-mo,*
ahl ah-nee-moh, ahl ah-nee-moh,

② *¿con qué se‿ha-ce‿el di-ne-ro?*
kohn keh seh‿ah-seh‿ehl dee-neh-roh?

③ *Al á-ni-mo, al á-ni-mo,*
ahl ah-nee-moh, ahl ah-nee-moh,

④ *con cás-ca-ra de hue-vo.*
kohn kah-skah-rah deh hweh-voh.

Pronunciation Practice 33

El mes de abril (The Month of April)

Folk Song from Spain

Phrase ① *El mes de_a-bril lle-gó,*
ehl mehs deh-yah-breel yeh-goh,

② *y_el cu-cu ya can-tó:*
y_ehl koo-koo yah kahn-toh:

③ *Cu-cú, cu-cú,*
koo-koo, koo-koo,

④ *el cu-cu ya can-tó.*
ehl koo-koo yah kahn-toh.

PRONUNCIATION PRACTICE 34

Hama chi dori (Plovers)

School Song from Japan
Music by Ryutaro Hirota
Words by Meishu Kashima

Phrase ① *Aa o ii tsu ki yo no*
ah oh ee tsoo kee yoh noh

② *ha ma be ni wa*
hah mah beh nee wah

③ *oh ya wo sa ga shi te*
oh yah oh sah gah shee deh

④ *na ku to ri ga.*
nah koo toh dee gah.

⑤ *Na mi no ku ni ka ra*
nah mee noh koo nee kah rah

⑥ *U ma re de ru*
oo mah reh deh roo

⑦ *Nu re ta tsu ba sa no*
noo reh tah tsoo bah sah noh

⑧ *ghi n no i ro.*
gee (n) noh ee roh.

PRONUNCIATION PRACTICE 35

El sapito (The Little Toad)

Music by Wilbur Alpírez Quesada
Words by José Sebastian Tallón

Phrase ① *Na-die sa-be don-de vi-ve,*
nah-dee‿eh sah-beh dohn-deh vee-veh,

② *en la ca-sa no lo vió,*
ehn lah kah-sah noh-loh vee‿oh,

③ *pe-ro to-dos lo‿es-cu-cha-mos,*
peh-roh toh-dohs loh‿ehs-koo-chah-mohs,

④ *el sa-pi-to glo, glo, glo.*
ehl sah-pee-toh gloh, gloh, gloh.

⑤ *Vi-vi-rá‿en la chi-me-ne-a?*
vee-vee-rah‿ehn lah chee-meh-neh-ah?

⑥ *Vi-ve‿o-cul-to‿en u-na flor?*
vee-veh‿oh-kool-toh-ehn oo-nah flohr?

⑦ *Don-de can-ta cuan-do llue-ve?*
dohn-deh kahn-tah kwahn-doh yoo‿eh-veh?

⑧ *el sa-pi-to glo.*
ehl sah-pee-toh gloh.

PRONUNCIATION PRACTICE 36

Don Gato

Folk Song from Mexico

Verse 1

Phrase ① *El se-ñor Don Ga-to es-ta-ba*
ehl seh-nyohr dohn gah-toh ehs-tah-bah

② *sen-ta-di-to en el te-ja-do*
sehn-tah-thee-toh ehn ehl teh-hah-doh

③ *cuan-do le vi-nie-ron car-tas, mia-rra-miau,*
kwahn-doh leh vee-nee eh-rohn kahr-tahs, mee yah-rrah-mee yow,

④ *cuan-do le vi-nie-ron car-tas, mia-rra-miau,*
kwahn-doh leh vee-nee eh-rohn kahr-tahs, mee yah-rrah-mee yow,

⑤ *si que-rí-a ser ca-sa-do.*
see keh-ree-ah sehr kah-sah-doh.

Verse 2

Phrase ① *Con u-na ga-ti-ta blan-ca,*
kohn oo-nah gah-tee-tah blahn-kah,

② *so-bri-na de un ga-to par-do,*
soh-bree-nah deh oon gah-toh pahr-doh,

③ *que no la ha-bía más lin-da, mia-rra-miau,*
keh noh lah ah-bee yah mahs leen-dah, mee yah-rrah-mee yow,

④ *que no la ha-bía más lin-da, mia-rra-miau,*
keh noh lah ah-bee yah mahs leen-dah, mee yah-rrah-mee yow,

⑤ *en las ca-sas de a-quel ba-rri-o.*
ehn lahs kah-sahs deh ah-kehl bah-rree yoh.

Grade 3, Teacher Edition, page 352

A-35

Pronunciation Practice 36 (continued)

Verse 3

Phrase ① *Don Ga-to con la_a-le-grí-a,*
dohn gah-toh kohn lah_ah-leh-gree_yah,

② *se_ha ca-í-do del te-ja-do;*
seh_ah kah-ee-doh dehl teh-hah-thoh;

③ *ha ro-to si-e-te co-sti-llas, mia-rra-miau,*
hah rroh-toh see_yeh-teh koh-stee-djahs, mee_yah-rrah-mee_yow,

④ *ha ro-to si-e-te co-sti-llas, mia-rra-miau,*
hah rroh-toh see_yeh-teh koh-stee-djahs, mee_yah-rrah-mee_yow,

⑤ *las dos o-re-jas y_el ra-bo.*
lahs dohs oh-reh-hahs ee_ehl rrah-boh.

Verse 4

Phrase ① *A vi-si-tar-lo ve-ní-an,*
ah vee-see-tahrr-loh veh-nee_yahn,

② *mé-di-cos y ci-ru-ja-nos*
meh-dee-kohs ee see-roo-hah-nohs

③ *to-dos di-cen que se mu-e-re, mia-rra-miau,*
toh-dohs dee-sehn keh seh moo-eh_rreh, mee_yah-rrah-mee_yow,

④ *to-dos di-cen que se mu-e-re, mia-rra-miau,*
toh-dohs dee-sehn keh seh moo-eh_reh, mee_yah-rrah-mee_yow,

⑤ *que Don Ga-to_es-tá muy ma-lo.*
keh dohn gah-toh_ehs-tah moo_ee mah-loh.

Grade 3, Teacher Edition, page 352

PRONUNCIATION PRACTICE 36 (CONTINUED)

Verse 5

Phrase ① *El ga-ti-to ya se‿ha muer-to,*
ehl gah-tee-toh yah seh‿ah moo‿ehr-toh,

② *ya se‿ha muer-to‿el buen Don Ga-to;*
yah seh‿ah moo‿ehr-toh‿ehl bwehn dohn gah-toh;

③ *a‿en-terr-ar ya se lo lle-van, mia-rra-miau,*
ah‿ehn-tehrr-ahrr yah seh loh djeh-vahn, mee‿yah-rrah-mee‿yow,

④ *a‿en-terr-ar ya se lo lle-van, mia-rra-miau,*
ah‿ehn-tehrr-ahrr yah seh loh djeh-vahn, mee‿yah-rrah-mee‿yow,

⑤ *to-dos los ga-tos llo-ran-do.*
toh-thohs lohs gah-tohs djoh-rrahn-doh.

Verse 6

Phrase ① *Cuan-do pa-sa-ba‿el en-ti-e-rro,*
kwahn-doh pah-sah-bah‿ehl ehn-tee-yeh-rroh,

② *por la pla-za del pes-ca-do,*
pohr lah plah-zah dehl pehs-cah-thoh,

③ *al o-lor de las sar-di-nas, mia-rra-miau,*
ahl oh-lohrr deh lahs sahrr-dee-nahs, mee‿yah-rrah-mee‿yow,

④ *al o-lor de las sar-di-nas, mia-rra-miau,*
ahl oh-lohrr deh lahs sahrr-dee-nahs, mee‿yah-rrah-mee‿yow,

⑤ *Don Ga-to‿ha re-su-ci-ta-do.*
dohn gah-toh‿ah rreh-soo-see-tah-thoh.

PRONUNCIATION PRACTICE 37

El barquito (The Tiny Boat)

Folk Song from Latin America

Verse 1

Phrase

① *Ha-bía_u-na vez*
ah-byou-nah vehs

② *un bar-co chi-qui-ti-co,*
oon bahr-koh chee-kee-tee-koh,

③ *Ha-bía_u-na vez*
ah-byou-nah vehs

④ *un bar-co chi-qui-ti-co,*
oon bahr-koh chee-kee-tee-koh,

⑤ *Ha-bía_u-na vez*
ah-byou-nah vehs

⑥ *un bar-co chi-qui-ti-co,*
oon bahr-koh chee-kee-tee-koh,

⑦ *Que no po-dí-a, que no po-dí-a,*
keh noh poh-dee-ah, keh noh poh-dee-ah,

⑧ *que no po-dí-a na-ve-gar.*
keh noh poh-dee-ah nah-veh-gahr.

⑨ *Pa-sa-ron u-na, dos, tres,*
pah-sa-rohn oo-nah, dohs, trehs,

⑩ *cua-tro, cin-co,*
kwah-troh, seen-koh,

⑪ *seis, sie-te se-ma-nas.*
says, syeh-teh seh-mah-nahs.

⑫ *Pa-sa-ron u-na, dos, tres,*
pah-sah-rohn oo-nah, dohs, trehs,

⑬ *cua-tro, cin-co,*
kwah-troh, seen-koh,

⑭ *seis, sie-te se-ma-nas.*
says, syeh-teh seh-mah-nahs

⑮ *Pa-sa-ron u-na, dos, tres,*
pah-sah-rohn oo-nah, dohs,
trehs,

⑯ *cua-tro, cin-co,*
kwah-troh, seen-koh,

⑰ *seis, sie-te se-ma-nas.*
says, syeh-teh seh-mah-nahs.

⑱ *Y el bar-qui-to, que no po-dí-a,*
ee ehl bahr-kee-toh,
keh noh poh-dee-ah,

⑲ *que no po-dí-a na-ve-gar.*
keh noh poh-dee-ah
nah-veh-gahr.

© PEARSON EDUCATION, INC.

Grade 3, Teacher Edition, page 358

PRONUNCIATION PRACTICE 38

El rabel (The Violin)

Folk Song from Chile

Verse 1

Phrase ① *El ra-bel pa-ra ser fi-no‿ha de ser de ver-de pi-no,*
ehl rah-behl pah-rah sehr fee-noh‿ah deh sehr deh vehr-deh pee-noh,

② *La vi-huela‿de du-ra he-bra y‿el se-dal de mu-la ne-gra,*
lah vee-weh‿lah deh doo-rah eh-brah ee‿ehl seh-dahl deh moo-lah neh-grah,

③ *La vi-huela‿de du-ra he-bra y‿el se-dal de mu-la ne-gra.*
lah vee-weh-‿lah deh doo-rah eh-brah ee‿ehl seh-dahl deh moo-lah neh-grah.

④ *An-da mo-re-ni-ta re-co-je‿e-se pa-ñue-lo.*
ahn-dah moh-reh-nee-tah reh-koh-heh eh-seh pah-nyoo-eh-loo.

⑤ *Mi-ra que‿es de se-da‿y lo‿a-rras-tras por el sue-lo.*
mee-rah keh‿ehs deh seh-dah‿ee loh‿ah-rrah-strahs pohr ehl sweh-loo.

PRONUNCIATION PRACTICE 39

Hevenu shalom aleichem
(We Come to Greet You in Peace)

Hebrew Folk Song

Phrase ① *He-ve-nu sha-lom a-lei-chem,*
heh-veh-noo shah-lohm ah-leh-hkhehm,

② *He-ve-nu sha-lom a-lei-chem,*
heh-veh-noo shah-lohm ah-leh-hkhehm,

③ *He-ve-nu sha-lom a-lei-chem,*
heh-veh-noo shah-lohm ah-leh-hkhehm,

④ *He-ve-nu sha-lom, sha-lom, sha-lom a-lei-chem.*
heh-veh-noo shah-lohm, shah-lohm, shah-lohm ah-leh-hkhehm.

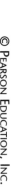

Grade 3, *Teacher Edition,* page 378

PRONUNCIATION PRACTICE 40

Hanuka, Hanuka

Words and Music by Flory Jagoda

Verse 1

Phrase ① *Ha-nu-ka, Ha-nu-ka,*
hkhah-noo-hkhah, hkhah-noo-hkhah,

② *O-cho di-yas di fe-li-si-ta.*
oh-choh dee-yahs dee feh-lee-see-tah.

③ *Ha-nu-ka, Ha-nu-ka,*
hkhah-noo-hkhah, hkhah-noo-hkhah,

④ *O-cho di-yas di fe-li-si-ta.*
oh-choh dee-yahs dee feh-lee-see-tah.

Verse 2

Phrase ① *Ha-nu-ka, Ha-nu-ka,*
hkhah-noo-hkhah, hkhah-noo-hkhah,

② *O-cho di-yas de kan-tar.*
oh-choh deh-yahs dee kahn-tahrr.

③ *Ha-nu-ka, Ha-nu-ka,*
hkhah-noo-hkhah, hkhah-noo-hkhah,

④ *O-cho di-yas de kan-tar.*
oh-choh deh-yahs dee kahn-tahrr.

PRONUNCIATION PRACTICE 40 (CONTINUED)

Verse 3

Phrase ① *Ha-nu-ka, Ha-nu-ka,*
hkhah-noo-hkhah, hkhah-noo-hkhah,

② *O-cho di-yas de ba-i-lar.*
oh-choh dee-yahs dee bah-ee-lahrr.

③ *Ha-nu-ka, Ha-nu-ka,*
hkhah-noo-hkhah, hkhah-noo-hkhah,

④ *O-cho di-yas de ba-yar.*
oh-choh dee-yahs dee bah-ee-yahrr.

Verse 4

Phrase ① *Ha-nu-ka, Ha-nu-ka,*
hkhah-noo-hkhah, hkhah-noo-hkhah,

② *O-cho di-yas de gu-zar.*
oh-choh deh-yahs dee goh-zahrr.

③ *Ha-nu-ka, Ha-nu-ka,*
hkhah-noo-hkhah, hkhah-noo-hkhah,

④ *O-cho di-yas de gu-zar.*
oh-choh deh-yahs dee goh-zahrr.

Grade 3, Teacher Edition, page 390

PRONUNCIATION PRACTICE 41

La piñata (The *Piñata*)

Folk Song from Mexico

Verse 1

Phrase ① *En las no-ches de po-sa-das,*
ehn lahs noh-chehs deh poh-sah-dahs,

② *La pi-ña-ta‿es lo me-jor:*
lah peen-yah-tah‿ehs loh meh-hohr:

③ *Aun las ni-ñas re-mil-ga-das*
own lahs neen-yahs reh-meel-gah-dahs

④ *Se‿an-i-man con gran fer-vor.*
seh‿ah-nee-mahn kohn grahn fehr-vohr.

Refrain

Phrase ① *Da-le, da-le, da-le,*
dah-leh, dah-leh, dah-leh,

② *no pier-das el ti-no.*
noh pyehr-dahs ehl tee-noh.

③ *Mi-de la dis-tan-cia*
mee-deh lah dees-than-syah

④ *que‿hay en el ca-mi-no.*
keh‿ah‿ee ehn ehl kah-mee-noh.

⑤ *Que si no le das*
keh see noh leh dahs

⑥ *de‿un pa-lo te em-pi-no,*
de‿oon pah-loh teh ehm-pee-noh,

⑦ *¡Por-que tie-nes au-ra*
pohr-keh tyeh-nehs ow-rah

⑧ *de pu-ro pe-pi-no!*
deh poo-roh peh-pee-noh!

© PEARSON EDUCATION, INC.

Verse 2

Phrase

① *Con tus o-ji-tos ven-da-dos*
kohn toos oh-hee-tohs vehn-dah-dohs

② *Y‿en las ma-nos un bas-tón;*
ee‿ehn lahs mah-nohs oon bahs-tohn;

③ *¡La‿o-lla róm-pe-la‿a pe-da-zos!*
lah‿oh-yah rohm-peh-lah‿ah peh-dah-sohs!

④ *¡No le ten-gas com-pa-sión!*
noh leh tehn-gahs kohm-pah-syohn!

PRONUNCIATION PRACTICE 42

Zumba, zumba

Folk Song from Spain

Refrain

Phrase ① *Zum-ba, zum-ba-le_al pan-de-ro*
soom-bah, soom-bah-leh_ahl pahn-deh-roh

② *al pan-de-ro y al ra-bel*
ahl pahn-deh-roh yahl rah-behl

③ *To-ca to-ca la zam-bom-ba*
toh-kah toh-kah lah sahm-bohm-bah

④ *da-le da-le_al al-mi-rez*
dah-leh dah-leh_ahl ahl-mee-rehs

Verse

Phrase ① *Es-ta no-che na-ce_un ni-ño*
eh-stah noh-cheh nah-seh_oon nee-nyoh

② *blan-co ru-bio_y co-lo-ra-do*
blahn-koh roo-bee_oh_ee koh-loh-rah-doh

③ *Que_ha de ser el pas-tor-ci-to*
keh_ah deh sehr ehl pah-stohr-see-toh

④ *pa-ra cui-dar el ga-na-do.*
pah-rah kwee-dahr ehl gah-nah-doh.

Aguinaldo

Carol from Puerto Rico

Phrase ① *Á-bre-me la puer-ta*
ah-breh-meh lah pwehrr-tah

② *Á-bre-me la puer-ta*
ah-breh-meh lah pwehrr-tah

③ *Que lo quie-ro_en-trar;*
keh loh kyeh-roh_ehn-trahrr;

④ *He_he-cho mis pas-te-les*
heh-choh mees pahs-teh-lehs

⑤ *Y_no quier-en que dar.*
ee_noh kyehrr-ehn keh thhahrr.

⑥ *He_he-cho mis pas-te-les*
heh-choh mees pahs-teh-lehs

⑦ *Y_no quier-en que dar.*
ee_noh kyehrr-ehn keh thhahrr.

Refrain
Phrase ① *A la sa-len-de-ra,*
ah lah sah-lehn-deh-rrah,

② *A la sa-len-de-ra,*
ah lah sah-lehn-deh-rrah,

③ *A la sa-len-de-ra,*
ah lah sah-lehn-deh-rrah,

④ *de mi co-ra-zón.*
deh mee koh-rrah-sohn.

Grade 3, Teacher Edition, page 402

PRONUNCIATION PRACTICE 43 (CONTINUED)

Verse 2

Phrase ① *Si no tie-ne na-da*
see noh tyeh-neh nah-thhah

② *Si no tie-ne na-da*
see noh tyeh-neh nah-thhah

③ *Na-da nos da-rá;*
nah-thah nohs dah-rrah;

④ *Pe-ro_lo que que-re-mos*
peh-roh_loh keh keh-rreh-mohs

⑤ *ca-ri-ño_y bon-dad.*
kah-ree-nyoh_ee bohn-thhahd.

⑥ *Pe-ro_lo que que-re-mos*
peh-roh_loh keh keh-rreh-mohs

⑦ *ca-ri-ño_y bon-dad.*
kah-ree-nyoh_ee bohn-thhahd.

PRONUNCIATION PRACTICE 44

Ichi-gatsu tsuitachi
(A New Year's Greeting)

School Song from Japan
Music by Ue Sanemichi

Phrase ① *To-shi no ha-ji-me no*
               toh-shee noh hah-zhyee-meh noh

        ② *Ta-me-shi to-te*
               tah-meh-shee toh-teh

        ③ *O-wa-ri na-ki yo no*
               oh-wah-ree nah-kee yoh noh

        ④ *Me-de-ta-sa o*
               meh-deh-tah-sah oh

        ⑤ *Mat-su-ta-ke ta-te te*
               mah-tsoo-tah-keh tah-teh teh

        ⑥ *Ka-do go-to ni*
               kah-doh goh-toh nee

        ⑦ *I-wo kyo ko-so*
               ee-woh kyoh koh-soh

        ⑧ *Ta-no-shi-ke-re.*
               tah-noh-shee-keh-reh.

Grade 3, Teacher Edition, page 406

PRONUNCIATION PRACTICE 45

Phonetic Pronunciation for Choral Singing of Non-English Songs

ah	as in f<u>a</u>ther	(m)	French nasal <u>m</u>, not articulated as a distinct letter but as an open nasal sound
ah_ee	as in l<u>i</u>ght (diphthong; a long *ah* sound with a hint of *ee* at close)		
		n	as in <u>n</u>ote
aw	as in <u>awe</u>	(n)	French nasal <u>n</u>, not articulated as a distinct letter, but as an open nasal sound
eh_ee	as in d<u>ay</u> (diphthong; a long *eh* sound with a hint of *ee* at close)		
		(ng)	as in sa<u>ng</u> (sometimes sounded as a prolonged nasal tone)
b	as in <u>b</u>utton		
ch	as in <u>ch</u>urch	oh	as in t<u>o</u>ne
d	as in <u>d</u>ad	oo	as in sp<u>oo</u>n
dj	as in ju<u>dg</u>e	ow	as in p<u>ow</u>der
ee	as in s<u>ee</u>d	p	as in <u>p</u>at
eh	as in l<u>e</u>t	r	as in <u>r</u>an
ew	used for French u (pronounce a bright *ee* and round the lips as if to whistle)	(r)	as in tu<u>r</u>n (combined with another vowel sound in German)
		rr	rolled <u>r</u>
f	as in <u>f</u>ace	rrrr	extended trilled <u>r</u>
g	as in <u>g</u>oat	s	as in <u>s</u>ong
h	as in <u>h</u>at	t	as in <u>t</u>ell
hkh	guttural, aspirant <u>h</u> of German, Hebrew <u>ch</u>, and Spanish <u>j</u>	th	as in <u>th</u>at
		thh	as in fea<u>th</u>er
ih	as in f<u>i</u>t	uh	as in <u>u</u>p
I	as in l<u>i</u>ght (a harsh *i* sound, where possible an *ah_ee* has been suggested for singing the I sound)	v	as in <u>v</u>an
		w	as in <u>w</u>ay
		wh	as in <u>wh</u>at
k	as in <u>k</u>ite	y	as in <u>y</u>es (not a vowel sound)
l	as in <u>l</u>et	z	as in <u>z</u>one
ll	prolonged <u>l</u> sound	zh	as in a<u>z</u>ure
m	as in <u>m</u>an		

Teacher Notes

ASSESSMENT

Table of Contents

ASSESSMENT

ASSESSMENT 1: UNIT 1

Show What You Know!

Sing this pattern with rhythm syllables first. Then **sing** the pitch syllables. Now **sing** the words while you **play** the pattern on a xylophone.

mi   mi   mi   mi   re   mi   do
dig - gi - dig - gi, ding dang dong.

Show What You Know!

- Add pitch syllables to these phrases to **create** your own pentatonic song.

- Use the pitches *do, re, mi, so,* and *la.*

- To make the song sound complete, the last pitch must be *do.* End the other phrases on a different pitch.

Sing your compositions or **play** them on a mallet instrument.

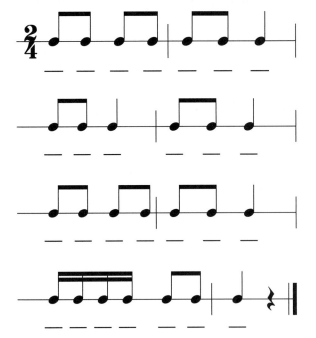

Grade 3, Teacher Edition, pages 15 and 31

ASSESSMENT 1: UNIT 1 (CONTINUED)

Review, Assess, Perform, Create

What Do You Know?

1. Look at the first line of "*Au clair de la lune*" below.

   a. Circle two pitches that show the melody moving up.

   b. Circle two pitches that show the melody moving down.

   c. Circle two pitches that show the melody repeating.

2. Which of these patterns shows AB form? Circle the letter of the correct answer.

   a. ○□○   **c.** ○□

   b. ○○   **d.** ○□△

ASSESSMENT 1: UNIT 1 (CONTINUED)

 **What Do You Hear? 1**   **Melodic Contour**

You will hear five musical examples. Does the end of each phrase move upward, move downward, or stay the same? Circle your answers.

1. upward   downward   same

2. upward   downward   same

3. upward   downward   same

4. upward   downward   same

5. upward   downward   same

What You Can Do

Sing and Move with Expression

Sing "I Don't Care If the Rain Comes Down" on page 24.

- Sing the first two lines *piano*. Use small steady-beat movements as you sing.

- Sing the last two lines *forte*. Use large steady-beat movements as you sing.

Grade 3, Teacher Edition, pages 42 and 43

ASSESSMENT 1: UNIT 1 (CONTINUED)

Rhythmic Ostinatos

Sing "Ding, Dong, Diggidiggidong" on page 14 with the recording. Softly pat one of these three ostinatos as you sing.

a.

b.

c.

Create a Melody

Create a melody for the poem "Rain," using ♩, ♫, and 𝄽.

• Use these pitches.

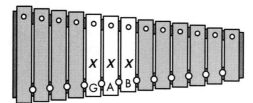

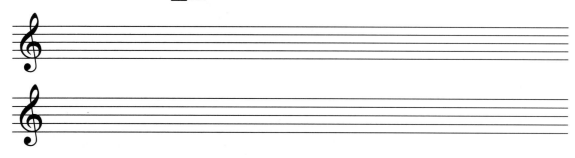

• Teach your friends to sing your melody.

ASSESSMENT 2: UNIT 2

Clap and say these patterns with rhythm syllables. Then **play** each one on percussion instruments with *"Ahora voy a cantarles."*

Sing each example with pitch syllables and hand signs. Write the pitch syllables in the spaces below the notes. Then **play** the notes on resonator bells.

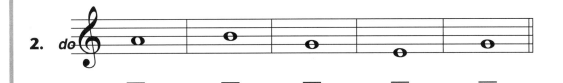

© PEARSON EDUCATION, INC.

Grade 3, Teacher Edition, pages 57 and 71

ASSESSMENT 2: UNIT 2 (CONTINUED)

Review, Assess, Perform, Create

What Do You Know?

1. Match the Italian musical terms with the correct definitions. Write the letters of your answers in the spaces provided.

___ *adagio*   **a.** speed of the beat

___ *allegro*   **b.** slow

___ tempo   **c.** moderate (medium)

___ *moderato*   **d.** fast

2. Look at these patterns. Decide if each one is moving by step, skip, or repeated tone. Write an "X" in front of each correct answer.

a.

___ step
___ skip
___ repeated tone

b.

___ step
___ skip
___ repeated tone

c.

___ step
___ skip
___ repeated tone

d.

___ step
___ skip
___ repeated tone

e.

___ step
___ skip
___ repeated tone

ASSESSMENT 2: UNIT 2 (CONTINUED)

What Do You Hear? 2   Identifying Tempo

Listen to four musical examples. Circle the word that describes the tempo of each example.

1.   *accelerando*   *ritardando*
2.   *allegro*   *adagio*
3.   *allegro*   *adagio*
4.   *accelerando*   *ritardando*

What You Can Do

Sing an Echo

Sing "I'm on My Way" on page 76 with half the class singing the first part and the other half singing the echo. Be sure to hold, or sustain, the long notes.

Perform a Call and Response

Perform this call-and-response speech piece with your classmates.

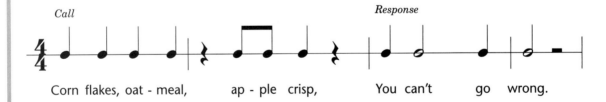

Corn flakes, oat - meal, ap - ple crisp, You can't go wrong.

Tur - nips, broc - co - li, rut - a - bag - a, peas, Make me grow strong!

ASSESSMENT 2: UNIT 2 (CONTINUED)

Create a Melody

Turn your speech piece into a song!

Create a melody for your call-and-response piece. Use the pitches marked below. Write the pitch names below the rhythmic notation.

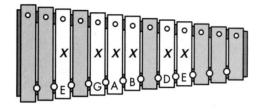

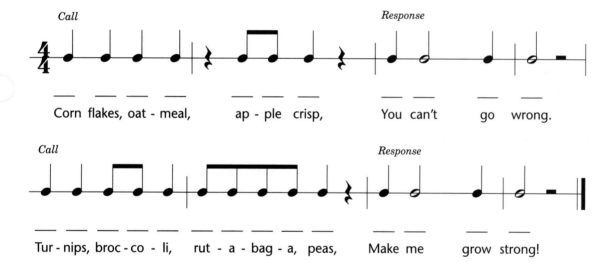

Corn flakes, oat - meal,   ap - ple crisp,   You can't   go   wrong.

Tur - nips, broc - co - li,   rut - a - bag - a, peas,   Make me   grow strong!

Assessment 3: Unit 3

Create your own four-bar rhythmic ostinato, using any of the rhythms below. **Play** your ostinato on percussion instruments as you **sing** "Love Somebody."

Which of the following rhythms last for one beat? Which rhythms last for two beats? Write the numeral 1 or 2 below each rhythm.

1.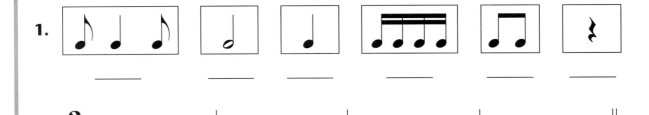

2.

Sing this ostinato using pitch syllables and hand signs. Try it in two groups. Half of the class will sing the ostinato while the other half sings "Alabama Gal," on page 106. Write the pitch syllables below each note.

Play the pitches of the ostinato on a xylophone while the rest of the class sings "Alabama Gal."

© PEARSON EDUCATION, INC.

ASSESSMENT 3: UNIT 3 (CONTINUED)

Review, Assess, Perform, Create

What Do You Know?

1. You're the composer, and you're making decisions about how you want your string quartet to sound. Circle the correct word.

    a. If you want the musicians to play so that the notes sound short or separated, tell them to play

                1) *legato.*   2) *staccato.*

    b. If you want the musicians to play so that the notes sound connected and smooth, tell them to play

                1) *legato.*   2) *staccato.*

    c. If you want the music to sound *staccato*, tell them to play

                1) *arco.*   2) *pizzicato.*

    d. For *legato* sounds, ask them to play

                1) *arco.*   2) *pizzicato.*

2. Read these rhythms. Which ones last for one beat? Circle your answers.

    a.   **b.**   **c.**   **d.**   **e.**

ASSESSMENT

Assessment 3: Unit 3 (continued)

What Do You Hear? 3   Identifying Instruments

You will hear three examples of string instruments. Circle the picture that matches the instrument you hear.

1.

string bass

viola

2.

string bass

viola

3.

viola

violin

What You Can Do

Move with the Music

Listen to the recording of *Gavotte* on page 88. Move to match each section of the piece. Use short movements for the *staccato* sections and smooth movements for the *legato* section.

Grade 3, Teacher Edition, pages 118 and 119

Assessment 3: Unit 3 (continued)

Create an Ostinato

Create a simple rhythm ostinato to accompany "*Hwa yuan li-de young wa wa*" on page 102.

• Choose from these rhythms for your four-beat ostinato.

• Perform your ostinato softly using body percussion as you sing.

• Then perform your ostinato on nonpitched percussion instruments. Choose instruments with timbres that match the song.

Improvise a Melody

Improvise a melody for your rhythm ostinato. Use these pitches. Begin and end on F or C.

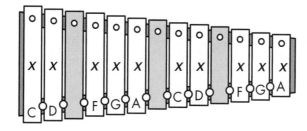

ASSESSMENT

ASSESSMENT 4: UNIT 4

Show What You Know!

Practice saying the rhythms below with rhythm syllables. Then **perform** them with two classmates. Which of these rhythms has an upbeat? Circle the upbeat.

Show What You Know!

1. Here are all of the pitches you know. **Sing** from *do* to *high do* and back again.

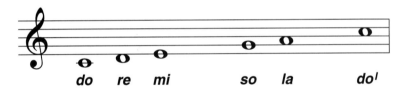

2. Where is *high do*? For each *do,* place a note on the staff where you would expect to find *high do*. Use the first example as a guide.

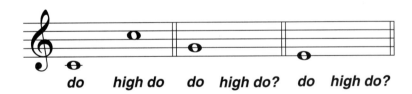

3. Look back! Find the *high do* in one of these songs. **Sing** the phrases that include *high do* using pitch syllables.

"Li'l Liza Jane," page 140
"Hop Up, My Ladies," page 142

ASSESSMENT 4: UNIT 4 (CONTINUED)

Review, Assess, Perform, Create

What Do You Know?

1. Look at the notation for "Hop Up, My Ladies" on page 142.

    a. How many times do the following pitches occur in the music? Write your answers next to the pitch syllables.

    so _____

    la _____

    mi _____

    re _____

    do¹ _____

    b. How many bar lines are in the music? _____

    c. How many double bar lines are in the music? _____

2. *Subito* means

    a. fast   **b.** sudden   **c.** gradual

3. Which mallet instruments below have bars made of wood? Which ones have bars made of metal? Write an "X" in front of the correct answers.

    a. xylophone   ___ wood

                       ___ metal

    b. marimba   ___ wood

                       ___ metal

    c. vibraphone   ___ wood

                       ___ metal

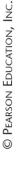

ASSESSMENT

ASSESSMENT 4: UNIT 4 (CONTINUED)

What Do You Hear? 4   Timbre

You will hear three different mallet instruments. Decide which instrument is featured in each example. Circle your answers.

1.

xylophone

marimba

vibraphone

2.

xylophone

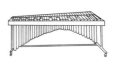
marimba

vibraphone

3.

xylophone

marimba

vibraphone

What You Can Do

Sing a Partner Song

Sing "Each of Us Is a Flower" on page 154. First, everyone sings the **A** section followed by the **B** section. Then sing both sections at the same time with a different group singing each section. Always sing with a good vocal quality. Make sure that both melodies are heard when they are sung together.

Create Music

Create an introduction and a *coda* for "Each of Us Is a Flower."

• Choose a rhythm pattern from the song to use in your introduction and *coda.*

• What instruments will you use to match the style of the song?

Grade 3, Teacher Edition, pages 156 and 157

ASSESSMENT 5: UNIT 5

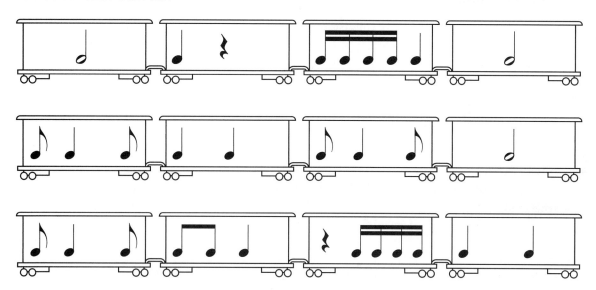

Say the rhythms below, using rhythm syllables. How many beats are in each train car? Write your answers below each train car.

Each of the melodies below is from a song you know. Circle the home tone in each example.

ASSESSMENT

ASSESSMENT 5: UNIT 5 (CONTINUED)

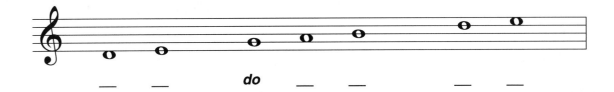

What Do You Know?

1. Name these pitches using pitch syllables. Write your answers below the notes.

_____   _____   *do*   _____   _____   _____   _____

2. Which of these patterns shows AABA form? Circle the correct answer.

a. ○□△△   **b.** ○□○○   **c.** ○○□○

Assessment 5: Unit 5 (continued)

What Do You Hear? 5A   Naming Instruments

Review the Sound Bank recordings of the instruments listed below. You will then hear three examples of different wind instruments. Circle the name of the instrument you hear.

1.   **a.** flute   **b.** panpipes

2.   **a.** *shakuhachi*   **b.** flute

3.   **a.** trumpet   **b.** tuba

What Do You Hear? 5B   Identifying Meter

You will hear two musical examples. Pat a steady beat to discover which is in $\frac{2}{4}$ meter and which is in $\frac{3}{4}$ meter. Circle your answers.

1.   **a.** $\frac{2}{4}$ **b.** $\frac{3}{4}$

2.   **a.** $\frac{2}{4}$ **b.** $\frac{3}{4}$

What You Can Do

Create a Canon

Create a speech canon. Work with a partner to write a four-line poem.

- Give lines 1 and 3 the same number of syllables.

- Give lines 2 and 4 the same number of syllables and make them rhyme.

- Decide where the second part of the canon should begin.

- Perform your speech canon for the class. Each of you can perform one part of the canon.

Assessment 6: Unit 6

Create a body percussion ostinato to perform with each rhythm below. Show upbeats and downbeats. How many beats are in each measure?

1.

2.

3.

Sing each of these melodies with pitch syllables. Write the pitch syllables below the notes. Circle the tonal center in each melody.

1.

2.

3.

Grade 3, Teacher Edition, pages 207 and 217

ASSESSMENT 6: UNIT 6 (CONTINUED)

What Do You Know?

1. Write the correct number of quarter notes to complete each measure.

2. Write each set of letter names below in the blanks provided. What words do they spell?

3. Match each vocabulary word to its definition. Write your answers in the spaces provided.

   a. *crescendo*   ___ gradually get softer

   b. *decrescendo*   ___ two or more pitches sound at the same time

   c. rondo   ___ gradually get louder

   d. harmony   ___ **A** section repeats between two or more
                                         different sections

Assessment 6: Unit 6 (continued)

What Do You Hear? 6   **Listening for Dynamics**

You will hear three selections. Circle the word that describes the dynamics you hear.

1.   *crescendo*   *decrescendo*

2.   *crescendo*   *decrescendo*

3.   *crescendo*   *decrescendo*

What You Can Do

Play Chords

Look at the notation for "Sweet Potatoes" on page 228.

- Find the chords marked in the notation.
- Strum the chords on Autoharp as you sing.
- Create a one-measure rhythm pattern.
- Strum the chords, using your created rhythm, as the class sings the song.

Grade 3, Teacher Edition, pages 232 and 233

ASSESSMENT 6: UNIT 6 (CONTINUED)

Create a Rondo

You can create your own rondo.

- Create a four-line poem to use as an **A** section.

- Create a **B** section and a **C** section.

- Use body percussion, instruments, or movement.

- Perform your sections in rondo form.

ASSESSMENT

ASSESSMENT: INTRODUCTION

Introduction for the Music Teacher

Checklists

Checklists are provided for performance skills (singing, playing instruments, reading, improvising, moving) and non-performance skills (composing/arranging/notating, listening). Have individual students demonstrate each of the items on the checklists. Guide the students in selecting music and tasks that will permit them to meet all of the goals outlined in the checklists.

You may consider assembling small ensembles in which students with different skill levels all perform a given piece together, but with students playing parts that are appropriate for their various skill levels. When reviewing students' work, continue to refer to the items on the checklists and point out ways their work does or does not meet each of the criteria. For students who do not perform as well as they are capable, provide opportunities to perform small sections of their pieces again. Have the students pay attention to one or two specific points that will improve their work. In this way, assessment becomes an important and contributing part of the learning process.

Rubrics

The rubrics are designed to be used together with the checklists. The goal of performance skills is for all students to perform well, regardless of the difficulty of the material they perform. The goal of non-performance skills is for all students to demonstrate competence, regardless of the difficulty of the composing, arranging, and listening tasks that they are assigned. Of course, some items on the checklists are more important than others, but all of them work together to create successful, expressive music performances, compositions, or informed listening experiences. If you wish to summarize your evaluations of the students' performances or work in a way that allows you to place each student or small group on a graded scale, you may use the rubrics for describing their performances or work.

Assessment: Performance Skills

Singing

Checklist for Singing
☐ Posture is upright and relaxed.
☐ Jaw and mouth are relaxed and open.
☐ Breath is inhaled with natural, relaxed expansion of the body.
☐ Tone is free, open, and even throughout range.
☐ Singing is accurate and in tune.
☐ Rhythm is precise and sung with inflection.
☐ Diction is clear (all words are understood).
☐ Volume level is balanced with other members of the ensemble.
☐ Dynamic and rhythmic variations are used to create expressive effects.

Rubric for Singing
☐ **Fluent** The student sings with fluency and ease. There are few errors. All items on the checklist are consistently demonstrated. The performance is confident, beautiful, and expressive.

☐ **Competent** The student sings with relative ease, but several errors or hesitations are present. Most items on the checklist are consistently demonstrated. The performance is confident and expressive.

☐ **More Practice Needed** The student has difficulty performing evenly and in time. Hesitations and errors are clearly evident. Only some of the checklist items are demonstrated. The performance does not convey the expressive intent of the piece performed.

ASSESSMENT: PERFORMANCE SKILLS

Playing Instruments

Checklist for Playing Instruments
❑ Posture is upright and relaxed.
❑ Instruments, sticks, and mallets (when used) are held loosely and comfortably.
❑ Arms, hands, and fingers move easily (no tension evident).
❑ Playing motion is efficient and smooth.
❑ Instrument tone is open, resonant, and even.
❑ Notes are performed accurately and in tune.
❑ Rhythm is accurate and precise.
❑ Tempo is steady and even.
❑ Volume level is balanced with other members of the ensemble.
❑ Dynamic and rhythmic variations are used to create expressive effects.

Rubric for Playing Instruments
❑ **Fluent** The student plays with fluency and ease. There are few errors. All items on the checklist are consistently demonstrated. The performance is confident, beautiful, and expressive.

❑ **Competent** The student plays with relative ease, but several errors or hesitations are present. Most items on the checklist are consistently demonstrated. The performance is confident and expressive.

❑ **More Practice Needed** The student has difficulty performing evenly and in time. Hesitations and errors are clearly evident. Only some of the checklist items are demonstrated. The performance does not convey the expressive intent of the piece performed.

ASSESSMENT: PERFORMANCE SKILLS

Reading

*Checklist for Reading
* ❏ Selects appropriate tempo at which to perform unfamiliar music.
* ❏ Identifies passages that are not immediately interpretable or technically difficult.
  ❏ Rehearses difficult or unfamiliar elements in isolation.
  ❏ Pitches are performed accurately.
  ❏ Rhythm is accurate and precise.
  ❏ Rhythm is performed with appropriate inflection.
  ❏ Style of articulation (if applicable) is accurate and consistent.
  ❏ Dynamic levels are accurate.
  ❏ Tempo is steady and even when appropriate.
  ❏ Rhythmic and dynamic variations are used to create expressive effects.

* Refer to tasks involved in learning unfamiliar music.

Rubric for Reading
❏ Fluent The student reads with fluency and ease. There are few errors. All items on the checklist are consistently demonstrated. The performance is confident, beautiful, and expressive.

❏ Competent The student reads with relative ease, but several errors or hesitations are present. Most items on the checklist are consistently demonstrated. The performance is confident and expressive.

❏ More Practice Needed The student has difficulty performing evenly and in time. Hesitations and errors are clearly evident. Only some of the checklist items are demonstrated. The performance does not convey the expressive intent of the piece performed.

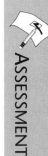

ASSESSMENT

ASSESSMENT: PERFORMANCE SKILLS

Moving and Improvising

Checklist for Moving
❑ Weight of the body is balanced and secure.
❑ Limbs move easily and without unnecessary tension.
❑ Movements depict the style of music (for example, rhythm, articulation).
❑ Movements are coordinated with the pulse of the music (if applicable).
❑ Changes in movements appropriately mirror changes in the music.
❑ Sizes and distances of movements are appropriate for the occasion and location (for example, on a dance floor, in a circle with classmates, or seated in a chair).

Checklist for Improvising
❑ Notes are grouped in discernible phrases.
❑ Repetition of melodic motives is used to extend and elaborate phrases.
❑ Individual phrases are unified by consistency and continuity.
❑ Phrases are organized with clear, balanced antecedents and consequents.
❑ Harmonic motion (when harmony is present) is logical.
❑ Dynamic and rhythmic variations are used to create expressive effects.
❑ Musical effects are consistent with the improviser's intent.

Rubric for Moving and Improvising
❑ **Fluent** The student moves or improvises with fluency and ease. There are few errors. All items on the checklist are consistently demonstrated. The performance is confident, beautiful, and expressive.

❑ **Competent** The student moves or improvises with relative ease, but several errors or hesitations are present. Most items on the checklist are consistently demonstrated. The performance is confident and expressive.

❑ **More Practice Needed** The student has difficulty performing evenly and in time. Hesitations and errors are clearly evident. Only some of the checklist items are demonstrated. The performance does not convey the expressive intent of the piece performed.

ASSESSMENT: NON-PERFORMANCE SKILLS

Composing/Arranging/Notating

Checklist for Composing/Arranging/Notating

❑ Instrument timbres and voice parts are combined effectively.
❑ Notes are grouped in phrases.
❑ Repetition of melodic motives is used to extend and elaborate phrases.
❑ Individual phrases are unified by consistency and continuity.
❑ Phrases are organized with clear, balanced antecedents and consequents.
❑ Harmonic motion (when harmony is present) is logical.
❑ Part-writing (if applicable) follows the conventions of the style of composition.
❑ Dynamic and rhythmic variations are used to create expressive effects.
❑ Musical effects are consistent with the intent of the composer or arranger.
❑ Musical sounds are accurately transcribed using formal, informal, or invented notation.
❑ Notation is clear and readable by others.

Rubric for Composing/Arranging/Notating

❑ **Fluent** The composition or arrangement is expressive, beautiful, and consistent with the intent of the composer or arranger. All items on the checklist are consistently demonstrated.

❑ **Competent** The composition or arrangement is well organized and consistent with the intent of the composer or arranger. Most items on the checklist are consistently demonstrated.

❑ **More Practice Needed** The composition or arrangement is somewhat organized and may not be consistent with the intent of the composer or arranger. Only some of the checklist items are demonstrated.

ASSESSMENT: NON-PERFORMANCE SKILLS

Listening

Checklist for Listening

The first four items on this checklist pertain to behavior while listening; the remaining four pertain to auditory discriminations explained after listening.

❑ Remains quiet (when appropriate) while listening to live or recorded music.
❑ Remains stationary (when appropriate) while listening to live or recorded music.
❑ Moves appropriately while listening to music (for example, tapping to the beat, dancing) in social settings where movement is appropriate.
❑ Acknowledges performers with applause (when appropriate).
❑ Describes the timbres of musical tones and labels instruments and voice parts.
❑ Describes the formal organization of sounds (for example, the use of repetition, melodic contour, motivic development).
❑ Describes the emotional effects that the music elicits from self and others.
❑ Describes possible functions of the music in cultural contexts.

Rubric for Listening Discrimination

❑ **Fluent** All aspects of the music are accurately described, and the observations about the music are informative and interesting. All items on the checklist are consistently demonstrated.

❑ **Competent** Most aspects of the music are accurately described, and the observations about the music are informative. Most items on the checklist are consistently demonstrated.

❑ **More Practice Needed** Aspects of the music are described, but some important information is inaccurate or omitted. Only some of the checklist items are demonstrated.

Assessment Answer Key

Unit 1 (Pages B-2 to B-5)

Show What You Know! (Rhythm)

Kodály-based rhythm syllables:
ti-ri-ti-ri ti-ti ta

What Do You Know?

1. a. A correct answer could include the last two beats of measure 1, *de la*; m.1 beat 4 to m.2 beat 1, *la lu-*; the first two beats of m.3, *mon a-*.

b. A correct answer could include m.2, *lu-ne*; the last beat of m.3 to beat 1 of m.4, *pier-rot*.

c. A correct answer could include the first two pitches in m.1 (*Au clair*).

2. c

What Do You Hear? 1

1. downward
2. upward
3. stays the same
4. upward
5. downward

Unit 2 (Pages B-6 to B-9)

Show What You Know! (Rhythm)

Kodály-based rhythm syllables:

1. *ta ti-ti ta ta ta-am ta*

2. *syn-co-pa ta ti-ti ta-am ta*

Show What You Know! (Melody)

1. *mi re do la₁ do*

2. *re mi do la₁ do*

3. *do re mi do la₁*

What Do You Know?

1. a. tempo

b. *adagio*

c. *moderato*

d. *allegro*

2. a. skip

b. step

c. repeated tone

d. skip

e. step

What Do You Hear? 2

1. *accelerando*

2. *allegro*

3. *adagio*

4. *ritardando*

Unit 3 (Pages B-10 to B-13)

Show What You Know! (Rhythm)

1. 2 2 1 1 1 1

Show What You Know! (Melody)

do mi do-la₁ so₁ so₁-so₁ la₁-la₁ do-do do

What Do You Know?

1. a. *staccato*

b. *legato*

c. *pizzicato*

d. *arco*

2. a. half note—2 beats

b. quarter note—1 beat

c. sixteenth notes—1 beat

d. quarter rest—1 beat

e. two eighth notes—1 beat

What Do You Hear? 3

1. viola

2. string bass

3. violin

Unit 4 (Pages B-14 to B-16)

Show What You Know! (Rhythm)

Kodály-based rhythm syllables:

1. *ta ta ta ta-a-am ta ta ta ta-a-am*

2. *ta ta ta ta ta ta ta ta ta ta-am ta*

3. *ta ta ta ta ta-am ta ta ta ta ta*

Number 3 has an upbeat. The upbeat is the first note of the exercise.

Show What You Know! (Melody)

What Do You Know?

1. a. *so* = 14; *la* = 17; *mi* = 21; *re* = 12; *high do* = 9

b. 31

c. 2

2. b

3. a. wood

b. wood

c. metal

What Do You Hear? 4

1. xylophone

2. marimba

3. vibraphone

ASSESSMENT ANSWER KEY (CONTINUED)

Unit 5 (Pages B-17 to B-19)

Show What You Know! (Rhythm)

Kodály-based rhythm syllables:
ta-am ta (rest) ti-ri-ti-ri ta ta-am
syn-co-pa ta ta syn-co-pa ta-am
syn-co-pa ti-ti ta (rest) ti-ri-ti-ri ta ta
There are two beats in each train car.

Show What You Know! (Melody)

1. home tone = F

2. home tone = C

3. home tone = C

What Do You Know?

1. *low so, low la, do, re, mi, so, la*

2. c

What Do You Hear? 5A

1. flute (western)

2. *shakuhachi*

3. tuba

What Do You Hear? 5B

1. $\frac{3}{4}$

2. $\frac{2}{4}$

Unit 6 (Pages B-20 to B-23)

Show What You Know! (Rhythm)

You will know how many beats to use for each ostinato by counting the number of beats in each example.

Show What You Know! (Melody)

1. *so, la, do re do la, so,* tonal center = *so,*

2. *la, la, do re mi do la,* tonal center = *la,*

3. *do la, do re mi re do* tonal center = *do*

What Do You Know?

1. Students should add a quarter note; two quarter notes; two quarter notes

2. FED; BAG; AGE

3. b. *decrescendo*

d. harmony

a. *crescendo*

c. rondo

What Do You Hear? 6

1. *crescendo*

2. *crescendo*

3. *decrescendo*

GRAPHIC ORGANIZERS

Table of Contents

GRAPHIC ORGANIZER

Graphic Organizer 1

Comparison

Alike	Different

GRAPHIC ORGANIZER 2

Information Organizer Chart

GRAPHIC ORGANIZER

KWHL Chart

What I know	
What I want to know	
How I will learn this	
What I learned	

GRAPHIC ORGANIZER 4

Semantic Feature Analysis

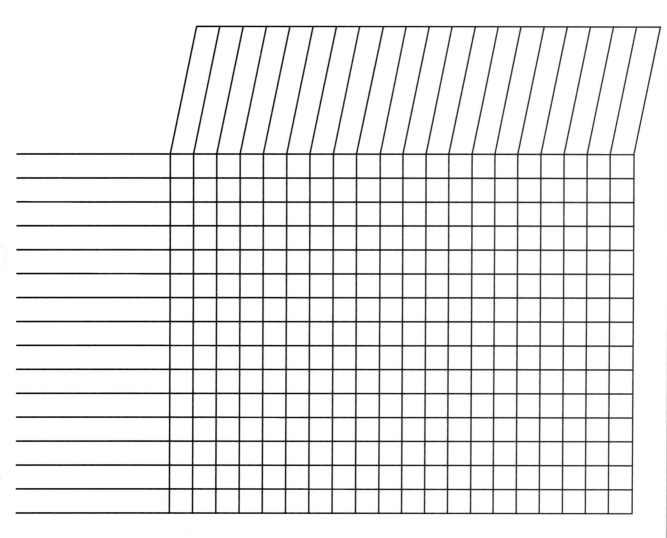

GRAPHIC ORGANIZER

GRAPHIC ORGANIZER 5

Semantic Map

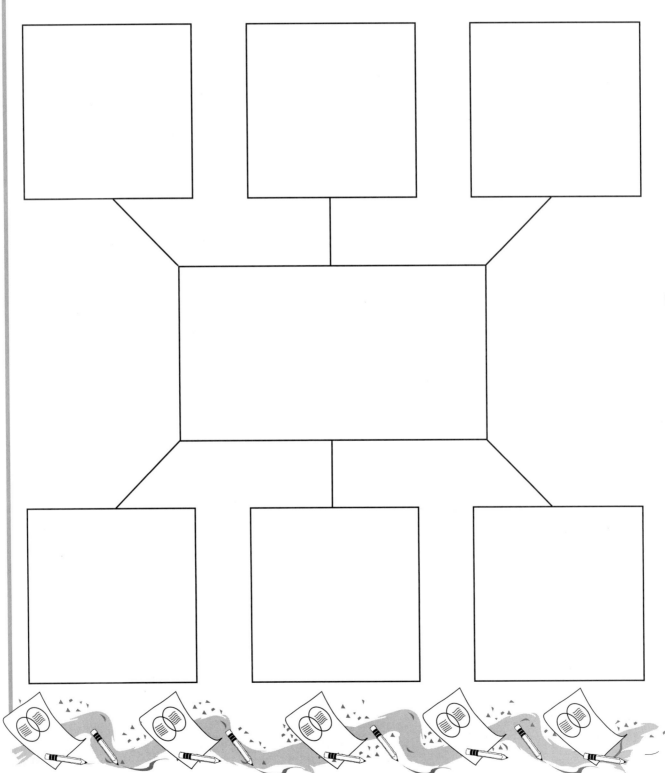

GRAPHIC ORGANIZER 6

Story Map

Title: _____

Setting
Characters:
Place:
Time:

▼

Problem:

▼

Events Leading to Resolution

▼

▼

▼

▼

Resolution:

GRAPHIC ORGANIZER 7

Venn Diagram

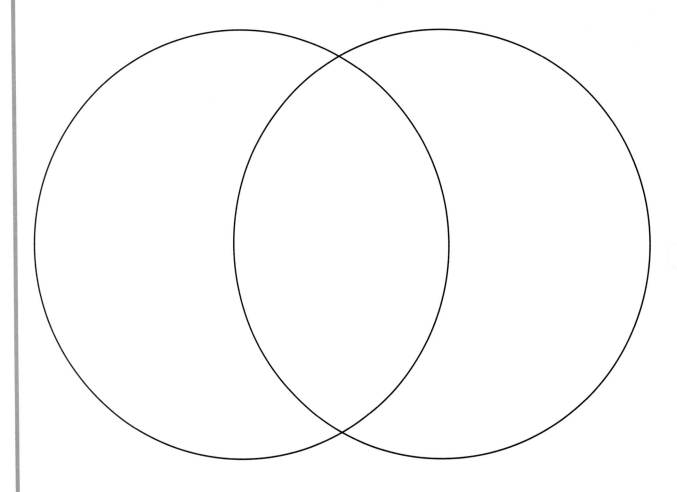

MUSIC READING WORKSHEETS
Table of Contents

Music Reading Worksheet 1

Writing Rhythms

Create your own gypsy rhythms by writing either ♩, ♫, or 𝄽 on each drum below.

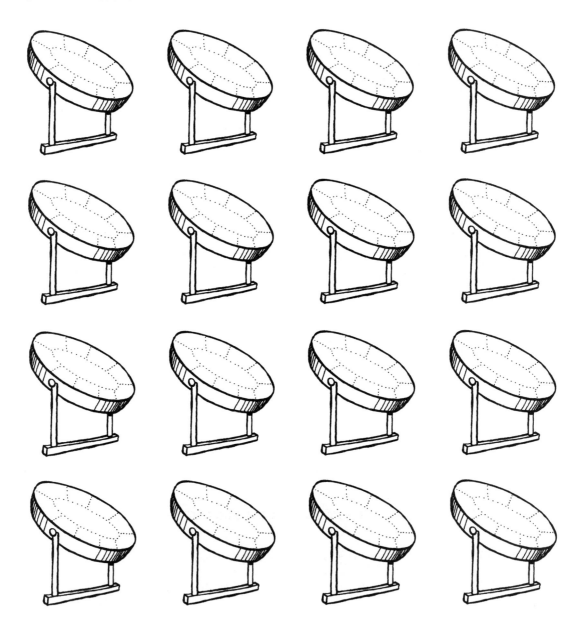

Grade 3, Teacher Edition, page 12

MUSIC READING WORKSHEET 2

Saying Rhythms

Say these rhythms using rhythm syllables.

Ding, Dong, Diggidiggidong

English Version Adapted by Margaret Murray
From Orff-Keetmen, Orff-Schulwerk, Vol. 1

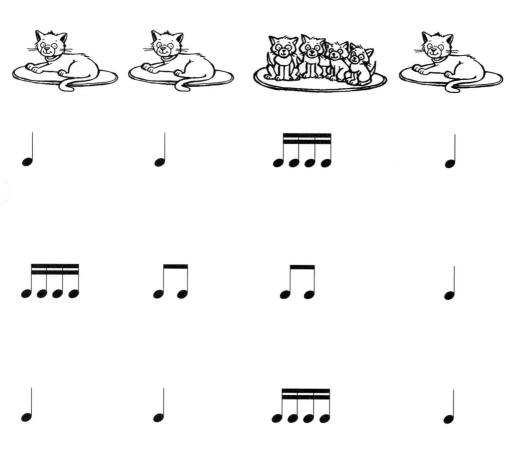

MUSIC READING WORKSHEET 3

Composing Your Own Song

Add *mi, re,* or *do* to the rhythms below to compose your own song. End on *do.*

Now write your song on the staff below.

MUSIC READING WORKSHEET 4

The Pentatonic Scale on the Staff

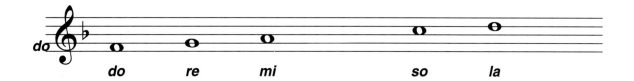

do   do   re   mi   so   la

Notice the new placement of *do* on the staff below.
Write the pitches shown above with the new *do*.

Notice the new placement of *do* on the staff below.
Write the pitches above with a new *do*.

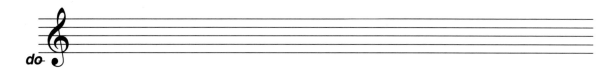

MUSIC READING WORKSHEET 5

Syncopation Study

Find the ties. Clap the rhythm.

Black Snake

Traditional

MUSIC READING WORKSHEET 5 (CONTINUED)

Fill in the blank measures to complete the rhythm for "Black Snake." Include the ties.

MUSIC READING WORKSHEET 6

Writing Pitches

Sing these pitch syllables and show hand signs.

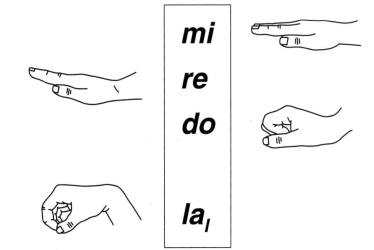

| mi |
| re |
| do |
| la, |

Write these pitches on the staff.

do

mi   re   do   la,

do

mi   re   do   la,

do

mi   re   do   la,

MUSIC READING WORKSHEET 7

Musical Form

Label the form below. Then create your own rhythms for the form shown at the bottom of the page. Use ♩, ♫, ‿, and ♬ when creating your rhythms.

Chicken on the Fence Post

Play-Party Song from the United States

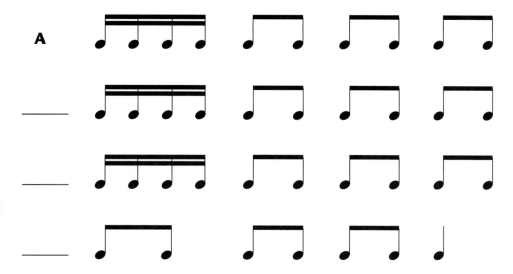

A

___

___

___

A

B

A

C

MUSIC READING WORKSHEET 8

Syncopation

Say and clap this rhythm.

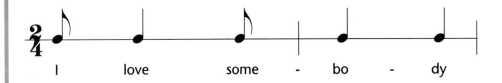

I   love   some - bo - dy

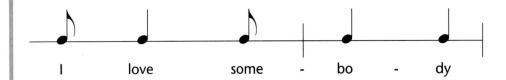

I   love   some - bo - dy

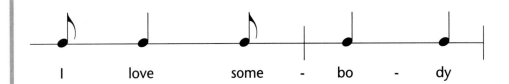

I   love   some - bo - dy

Yes,   I   do —!

MUSIC READING WORKSHEET 9

A New Note

Sing the notes below. Hum the new note.

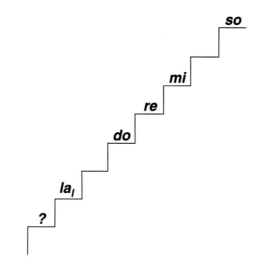

Write the new note on the staff.

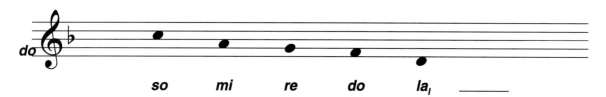

Music Reading Worksheet 10

Identifying Pitches

Write the missing pitch syllables under the rhythms.

Alabama Gal

Folk Song from Alabama

do   do   la,   do   ___   do   do   do   la,   ___

do   do   la,   do   mi   mi   so   mi   re   ___

MUSIC READING WORKSHEET 11

Dividing Music into Measures

Add bar lines to make complete measures. Remember to place a double bar line at the end.

The Juniper Tree

Folk Song from Arkansas

Oh, sis - ter Phoe - be, how mer - ry were we, The

night we sat un - der the ju - ni - per tree, The

ju - ni - per tree, hi - o, hi - o, The

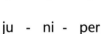

ju - ni - per tree, hi - o.

MUSIC READING WORKSHEET 12

Note Values

Find another way to write each of the rhythms below.

1.  =

2.  =

3. =

Use , , , , or to complete the empty measures.

Grade 3, Teacher Edition, page 132

Music Reading Worksheet 13

Writing Pitches

Sing the pitches on the ladder. Write each pitch on the staff.

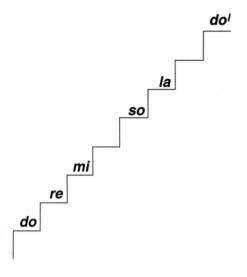

MUSIC READING WORKSHEET 14

Creating a Song

Use any of these notes (*do, re, mi, so, la, do¹*) to create a song.
Then sing your composition.

do   do¹   do¹   __   __   __   __   __   so

do   do¹   do¹   __   __   __   __   __   do

MUSIC READING WORKSHEET 15

Writing Rhythms

Write your own rhythms to create this rhythm train. Each railroad car should have two beats of rhythm.

Music Reading Worksheet 16

Filling in Notes

Fill in the notes on each staff to make a *do*-pentatonic scale. Sing each scale, then play each scale on a xylophone. Which scale is higher? lower?

1.

do   so₁   la₁   do   re   mi   so   la

2.

do   so₁   la₁   do   re   mi   so   la

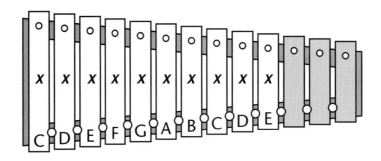

Grade 3, Teacher Edition, page 178

MUSIC READING WORKSHEET 17

Writing the Pentatonic Scale

Sing a *do*-pentatonic scale, then write the pitches on the staff. Play the scale up and down on a xylophone and create various rhythm patterns.

do

do re mi   so la   do*I*

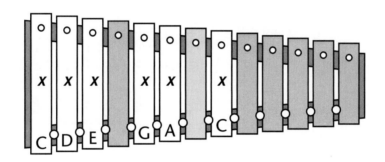

MUSIC READING WORKSHEET 18

Writing the *la*-Pentatonic Scale

Fill in the notes on the staff to make a *la*-pentatonic scale. Sing the scale, then play the scale on a xylophone.

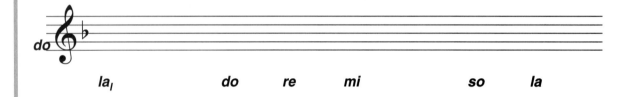

la₁   do   re   mi   so   la

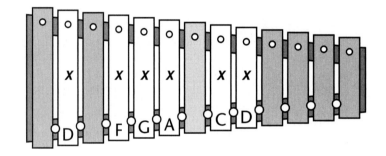

MUSIC READING WORKSHEET 19

Filling in Rhythms

Add rhythm patterns in the empty measures below. What is the meter? How many beats should be in each measure? Perform your composition on rhythm sticks or a drum.

MUSIC READING WORKSHEET 20

Finding the Upbeat

To help find the upbeats, place a bar line before each strong beat. Strong beats are marked with an x. Be sure to place a double bar at the end of each example.

1.

2.

3.

Grade 3, Teacher Edition, page 206

MUSIC READING WORKSHEET 21

Curwen Hand Signs

 high do (do¹)

 la

 so

 mi

 re

 do

Name _____ Class _____

Music Reading Worksheet 22

The Staff

MUSIC READING PRACTICE
Table of Contents

Recordings of the Reading Sequence exercises in this section are provided in the CD package.

© PEARSON EDUCATION, INC.

READING PRACTICE

MUSIC READING PRACTICE: SEQUENCE 1

Rhythm: Reading ♩, ♫, and 𝄽

Use rhythm syllables to **read** and **perform** these rhythms.

Alligator Pie

Rhythmic Setting by Edith Bicknell

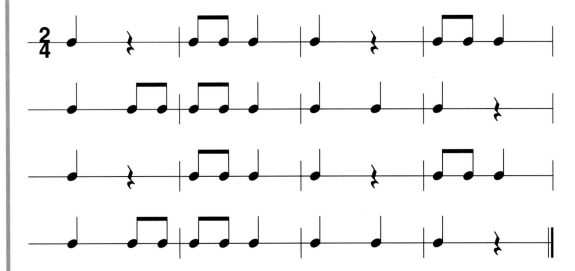

MUSIC READING PRACTICE: SEQUENCE 2

Rhythm: Reading ♪♫♫

Read and **perform** this exercise using rhythm syllables. Then **play** the rhythms on percussion instruments as you sing.

Ding, Dong, Diggidiggidong

From Orff-Keetman, Orff Schulwerk, Vol. 1

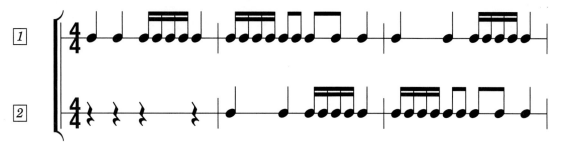

READING PRACTICE

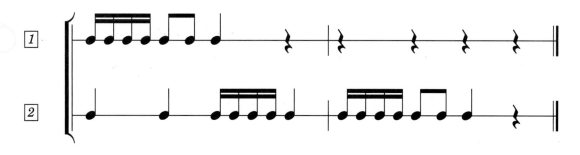

MUSIC READING PRACTICE: SEQUENCE 3

Melody: Reading *mi*, *re*, and *do*

Use pitch syllables to **read** and **sing** this melody with the refrain.

Oh, Won't You Sit Down

African American Spiritual

MUSIC READING PRACTICE: SEQUENCE 4

Melody: Reading *do*-Pentatonic

Read and **sing** this simple version to practice inner hearing.

Ida Red

Folk Song from Kentucky

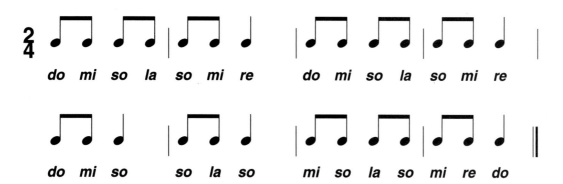

READING PRACTICE

MUSIC READING PRACTICE: SEQUENCE 5

Rhythm: Reading

Read and **perform** this exercise using rhythm syllables.

Black Snake

Traditional

Grade 3, Teacher Edition, page 52

Music Reading Practice: Sequence 6

Rhythm: Reading ♪ ♩ ♪

Read and **perform** this exercise using rhythm syllables.

Mister Ram Goat-O

Folk Song from Trinidad

Reading Practice

MUSIC READING PRACTICE: SEQUENCE 7

Melody: Reading *low la*

Use pitch syllables and hand signs to **read** and **sing** this exercise.

One Morning Soon

African American Spiritual

Grade 3, Teacher Edition, page 68

MUSIC READING PRACTICE: SEQUENCE **8**

Melody: Reading *low la*

Read and **sing** this melody using pitch syllables and hand signs.

Hosisipa

*Native American Game Song
of the Sioux*

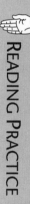

MUSIC READING PRACTICE: SEQUENCE 9

Rhythm: Reading ♩♫♫

Use rhythm syllables to **read** and **perform** these rhythms.

Chicken on the Fence Post

Play-Party Song from the United States

Grade 3, Teacher Edition, page 92

MUSIC READING PRACTICE: SEQUENCE 10

Rhythm: Reading  and

Read and **perform** this exercise using rhythm syllables. Then **play** the rhythms on percussion instruments as you sing.

Love Somebody

Folk Song from the United States

READING PRACTICE

MUSIC READING PRACTICE: SEQUENCE 11

Melody: Reading *low so*

Read and **sing** this exercise to practice inner hearing.

Hwa yuan li-de young wa wa
(Garden Lullaby)

Music by Chuen-Taur Su

MUSIC READING PRACTICE: SEQUENCE 12

Melody: Reading *low so*

Use pitch syllables and hand signs to **read** and **sing** this countermelody.

Alabama Gal

Folk Song from Alabama

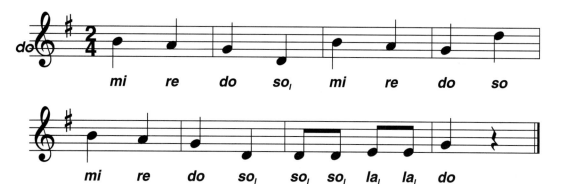

mi   re   do   so,   mi   re   do   so

mi   re   do   so,   so,   so,   la,   la,   do

READING PRACTICE

MUSIC READING PRACTICE: SEQUENCE 13

Rhythm: Reading

Read and **perform** these rhythms.

Morning Is Come

Round from England

© PEARSON EDUCATION, INC.

MUSIC READING PRACTICE: SEQUENCE 14

Rhythm: Reading Rhythms in $\frac{3}{4}$

Conduct a three-beat pattern as you sing. Then **read** and **perform** this exercise using rhythm syllables.

The Juniper Tree

Folk Song from Arkansas

"The Juniper Tree" Copyright 1937 by John A. Lomax. Reprinted by permission of Global Jukebox Publishing.

READING PRACTICE

MUSIC READING PRACTICE: SEQUENCE 15

Melody: Reading *high do*

Use pitch syllables and hand signs to **read** and **sing** this countermelody.

Li'l Liza Jane

Dance Song from the United States

MUSIC READING PRACTICE: SEQUENCE **16**

Melody: Reading *do* and *high do*

Read and **sing** this countermelody to practice inner hearing.

Hop Up, My Ladies

Folk Song from the United States

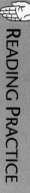

READING PRACTICE

$\frac{2}{4}$

do'   so   la   so   do   do'   do'   so

do'   so   la   so   re   re   mi   re

do'   so   la   so   do   do'   do'   so

do   do   re   mi   do   do'   do'   do'

MUSIC READING PRACTICE: SEQUENCE **17**

Rhythm: Reading Rhythms in $\frac{2}{4}$

Use rhythm syllables to **read** and **perform** these rhythms.

Don't Let Your Watch Run Down

Work Song from South Texas

MUSIC READING PRACTICE: SEQUENCE 18

Rhythm: Reading ¾ and ²⁄₄

Read and **perform** this exercise using rhythm syllables. Then **play** the rhythms on percussion instruments as you sing.

Coffee Grows on White Oak Trees

Folk Song from the United States

READING PRACTICE

MUSIC READING PRACTICE: SEQUENCE 19

Melody: Reading a *do*-Pentatonic Song

Read and **sing** this melody using pitch syllables and hand signs.

Don't Let the Wind   *Folk Song from St. Helena Island*

MUSIC READING PRACTICE: SEQUENCE **20**

Melody: Reading a *la*-Pentatonic Song

Use pitch syllables and hand signs to **read** and **sing** this countermelody.

Erdö, erdö de magos
(In the Silent Forest)

Folk Song from Hungary

la   so   mi   re   do   la,

la,   do   do   re   mi   re   do   do   mi

la,   do   do   re   mi   re   do   do   re

la   so   mi   re   do   la,

READING PRACTICE

MUSIC READING PRACTICE: SEQUENCE 21

Rhythm: Reading Rhythms in 4/4

Read and **perform** these rhythms.

Turn the Glasses Over

Folk Song from the United States

MUSIC READING PRACTICE: SEQUENCE 22

Rhythm: Reading Upbeats

Read and **perform** this exercise using rhythm syllables. Does it begin on an upbeat or a downbeat?

Hashkediya (*Tu b'Shvat* Is Here)

Music by M. Ravina

READING PRACTICE

MUSIC READING PRACTICE: SEQUENCE 23

Melody: Reading a *so*-Pentatonic Song

Read and **sing** this exercise to practice inner hearing using pitch syllables and hand signs.

Pretty Saro   *Folk Song from Kentucky*

so, la, do do la, so, do re mi so

so, la, do do la, do re re mi re

mi mi mi re do la, do la, do re

so, la, do do la, so, do do la, so,

MUSIC READING PRACTICE: SEQUENCE 24

Melody: Reading Letter Names B-A-G

Use pitch syllables and hand signs to **read** and **sing** this melody. Then sing it with letter names.

Hot Cross Buns (Version 1)

Folk Song from England

READING PRACTICE

Teacher Notes

ORFF

Table of Contents

ORFF

ORFF 1

I Don't Care If the Rain Comes Down

*Traditional Folk Song
from the United States
Arranged by Konnie Saliba*

© PEARSON EDUCATION, INC.

*For abbreviations of instruments, see Instrumentarium on page F-39.

ORFF 2

Oh, Won't You Sit Down

African American Spiritual
Arranged by Konnie Saliba

ORFF

ORFF 2 (CONTINUED)

ORFF 3

One Morning Soon

African American Spiritual
Arranged by Konnie Saliba

* = Play any 2 notes

ORFF 4

Old Texas

Cowboy Song from Oklahoma
Arranged by Konnie Saliba

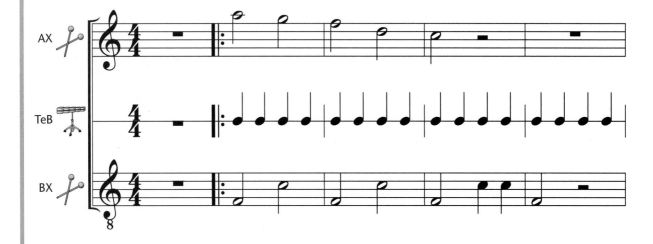

Grade 3, Teacher Edition, page 77

ORFF 5

Love Somebody

Folk Song from the United States
Arranged by Konnie Saliba

ORFF

ORFF 5 (CONTINUED)

Orff 6

Alabama Gal

Folk Song from Alabama
Arranged by Konnie Saliba

Stop on fermata on last verse.

Orff

ORFF 7

Old Man Mosie

Singing Game from the United States
Arranged by Julie Scott

ORFF 7 (CONTINUED)

ORFF

ORFF 8

Tender Shepherd

Music by Mark Charlap
Arranged by Paul Kerlee

When playing in canon, play the seventh measure two extra times to allow the second part to "catch up."

ORFF 9

The Groundhog Blues

Words and Music by Gayle Giese
Arranged by Konnie Saliba

ORFF

ORFF 10

Li'l Liza Jane

Dance Song from the United States
Arranged by Konnie Saliba

Grade 3, Teacher Edition, page 140

ORFF 10 (CONTINUED)

ORFF

ORFF 11

Hop Up, My Ladies

Folk Song from the United States
Arranged by Konnie Saliba

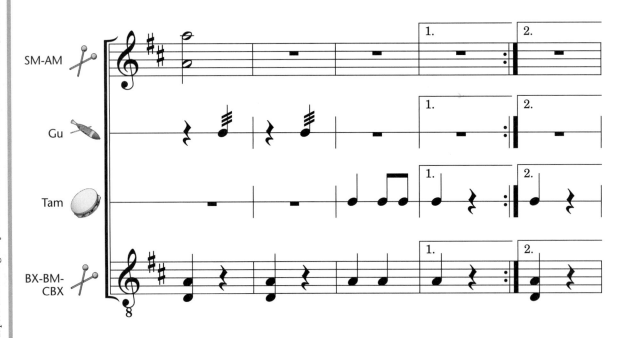

Grade 3, Teacher Edition, page 142

Orff 11 (continued)

ORFF

ORFF 11 (CONTINUED)

Grade 3, Teacher Edition, page 142

ORFF 12

Hush, Hush

African American Spiritual
Arranged by Konnie Saliba

ORFF

ORFF 12 (CONTINUED)

SX

AX

HD — *add more drums*

BX-BM

SX

AX

HD — *only one drum*

BX-BM

ORFF 13

Don't Let Your Watch Run Down

Work Song from South Texas
Arranged by Konnie Saliba

ORFF

ORFF 13 (CONTINUED)

SG-AG

AX-AM

BX-BM-CBX

Choose a nonpitched percussion instrument for each of the following words or phrases.

watch, down, Captain, Working' on the levee, day

Play the instrument whenever your "word" occurs.

ORFF 14

Now Let Me Fly

African American Spiritual
Arranged by Konnie Saliba

ORFF 14 (CONTINUED)

ORFF 15

Don't Let the Wind

Folk Song from St. Helena Island
Arranged by Konnie Saliba

ORFF

ORFF 15 (CONTINUED)

ORFF 16

Erdö, erdö de magos (In the Silent Forest)

Folk Song from Hungary
Arranged by Konnie Saliba

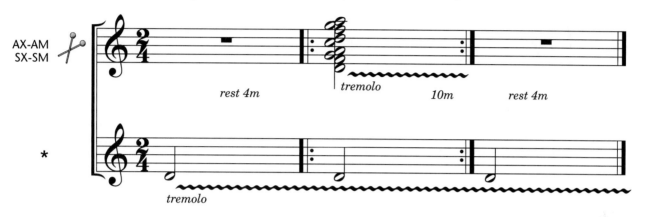

AX-AM
SX-SM

rest 4m   tremolo   10m   rest 4m

*

tremolo

Remove Es and Bs so instruments are in *la*-pentatonic on d.

AX-AM-SX-SM tremolo—choose any two notes

* improvised, nonpitched percussion—forest sounds like wind chimes—frogs (*guiro*) woodpecker (single temple block)

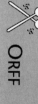

ORFF

ORFF 17

Turn the Glasses Over

Folk Song from the United States
Arranged by Konnie Saliba

Grade 3, Teacher Edition, page 204

ORFF 17 (CONTINUED)

ORFF

ORFF 18

Hashkediya (*Tu b'Shvat* Is Here)

Music by M. Ravina
Arranged by Konnie Saliba

Grade 3, Teacher Edition, page 206

ORFF **19**

A Ram Sam Sam

Folk Song from Morocco
Arranged by Danai Gagne

ORFF

ORFF 19 (CONTINUED)

ORFF 20

Pretty Saro

Folk Song from Kentucky
Arranged by Konnie Saliba

ORFF

Orff 21

Vamos a la mar (Let's Go to the Sea)

*Folk Song from Guatemala
Arranged by Paul Kerlee*

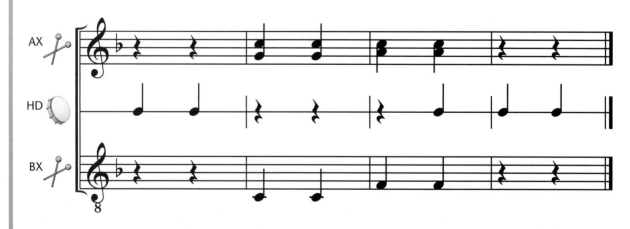

ORFF 22

*He's Got the Whole World
in His Hands*

African American Spiritual

ORFF 23

La paloma blanca
(The White Dove)

Folk Song from the Southwestern United States
Arranged by Konnie Saliba

ORFF 23 (CONTINUED)

ORFF

ORFF 24

El mes de abril (The Month of April)

Folk Song from Spain
Arranged by Konnie Saliba

Grade 3, Teacher Edition, page 328

ORFF 25

INSTRUMENTARIUM

Abbreviations of Instruments on a Score

Winds

SoR	Sopranino Recorder
SR	Soprano Recorder
AR	Alto Recorder
TR	Tenor Recorder
BR	Bass Recorder

Mallet Instruments

SG	Soprano Glockenspiel
AG	Alto Glockenspiel
SX	Soprano Xylophone
AX	Alto Xylophone
BX	Bass Xylophone
CBX	Contrabass Xylophone
SM	Soprano Metallophone
AM	Alto Metallophone
BM	Bass Metallophone

Percussion—Metals

Tr	Triangle
FC	Finger Cymbals
JB	Jingle Bells
CT	Chime Tree
AB	Agogo Bells
CB	Cow Bell
Cym	Cymbals
W	Slide Whistle

Percussion—Woods

WB	Wood Block
ToB	Tone Block
C	Castanets

Sh	Shakers
M	Maracas
Cb	Cabasa
R	Ratchet
Rt	Rattles
TeB	Temple Blocks
VS	Vibra Slap
Cl	Claves
Gu	Guiro
LD	Log Drum
SB	Sand Blocks
Af	Afuchi

Percussion—Membranes or Skins

HD	Hand Drum
Tam	Tambourine
BD	Bongo Drums
CD	Conga Drum
SD	Snare Drum

Large Percussion

HC	Hanging Cymbal
G	Gong
BD	Bass Drum

Tuned Instruments

G	Guitar
P	Piano
Tp	Timpani
DB	Double Bass

ORFF

Instrumentarium Diagram

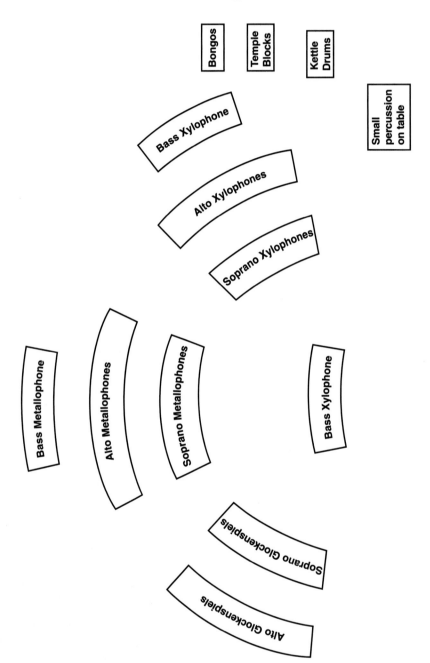

Bongos

Temple Blocks

Kettle Drums

Small percussion on table

Bass Xylophone

Alto Xylophones

Soprano Xylophones

Bass Metallophone

Alto Metallophones

Soprano Metallophones

Bass Xylophone

Soprano Glockenspiels

Alto Glockenspiels

Signing

Table of Contents

SIGNING 1

Name, Name, What's Your Name?

by Jim Solomon

name

Name,

name

name,

what

what's

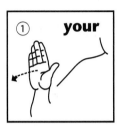

① **your**

your

name

name?

say

Say it

now

now,

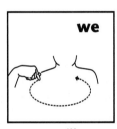

we

we'll

play

play a

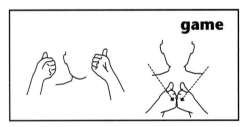

game

game.

say

Say it

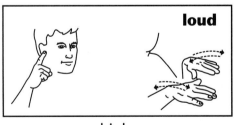

loud

high,

① palm out or directed toward specific person

SIGNING

SIGNING 1 (CONTINUED)

say

say it

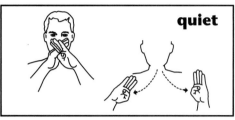

quiet

low,

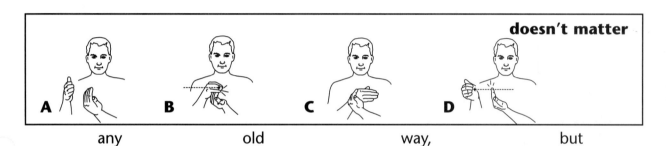

doesn't matter

A   B   C   D

any   old   way,   but

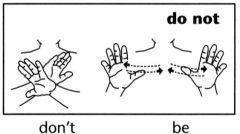

do not

don't   be

slow

slow.

In American Sign Language (ASL), when questions are asked that require a yes or no answer, the eyebrows are raised. When questions are asked that require other information, such as your name, the eyebrows are brought together.

SIGNING 2

Make New Friends

Traditional Round

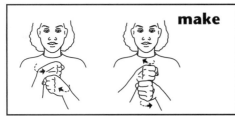

Make

new

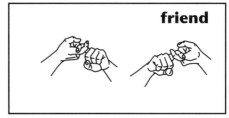

friends,

but keep

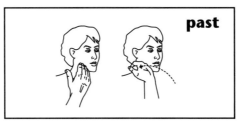

the old,

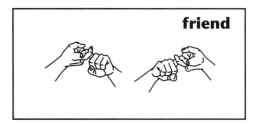

One

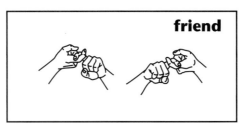

is

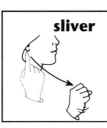

silver

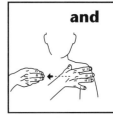

and the

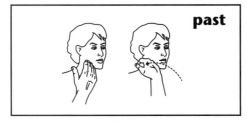

other

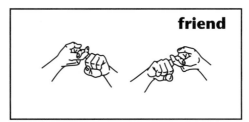

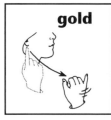

gold.

SIGNING 3

Train Is A-Comin'

African American Spiritual

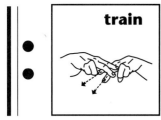
train
Train is a

come
comin',

yes
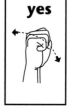
oh, yes,

train
Train is a

come
comin',

train
Train is a

come
comin',

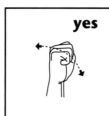
yes
oh, yes

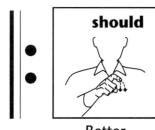
should
Better

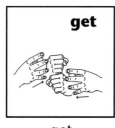
get
get

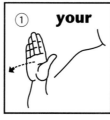
① **your**
your

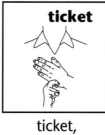
ticket
ticket,

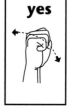
yes
oh, yes

① palm out or directed toward specific person

Signing 3 (continued)

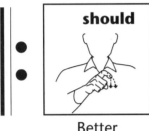

Better

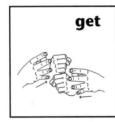

get

your

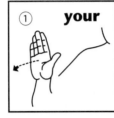

ticket,

Better

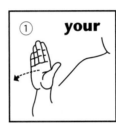

get

your

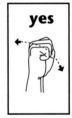

ticket,

oh, yes.

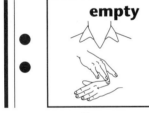

Room

for

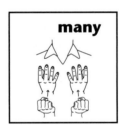

many

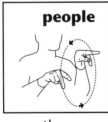

others,

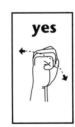

oh, yes,

Signing 3 (continued)

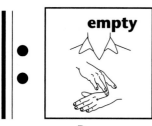
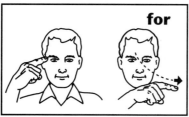

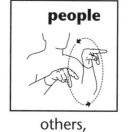

empty — Room **for** — for **many** — many **people** — others,

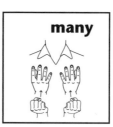

empty — Room **for** — for **many** — many

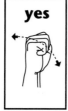

people — others, **yes** — oh, yes.

SIGNING 4

Black Snake

Traditional

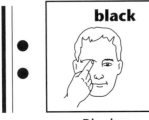
black

Black

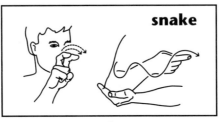
snake

snake,

black

black

snake

snake,

where

where are

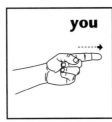
you ①

you

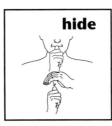
hide

hiding?

repeat 3 times

don't

Don't

you

you

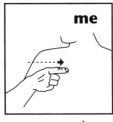
bite

bite

me

me!

① palm out, wiggle finger

© PEARSON EDUCATION, INC.

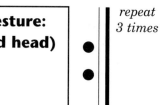

SIGNING 5

Love Somebody

Folk Song from the United States

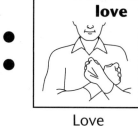   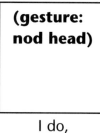

love	someone	yes	(gesture: nod head)	repeat 3 times
Love	somebody,	yes,	I do,	

 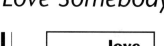

love	someone
Love some-	body but I

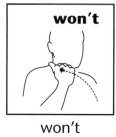  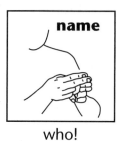

won't	tell	name
won't	tell	who!

For signs like *yes* or *no,* signers nod their head when signing *yes,* and shake their head when signing *no.*

For the sign *yes,* the fist represents the head nodding.

SIGNING 6

Hush, Hush

African American Spiritual

hush 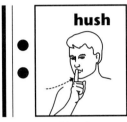	**hush** 	**someone** 	**call** 	① **my** 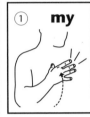	**name** 
Hush,	hush,	somebody's	callin'	my	name,

3 times

① **my** 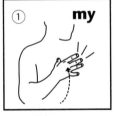	**Lord** 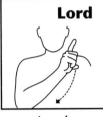	① **my** 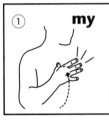	**Lord** 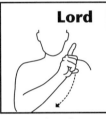	**what to do** 
Oh, my	Lord,	oh, my	Lord, what	shall I do?

who 	**who** 	**who** 	**Lord** 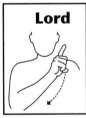	**call** 	① **my** 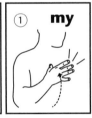	**name** 
Who,	who,	who,	Lord,	is callin'	my	name?

3 times

① **my** 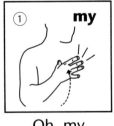	**Lord** 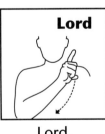	**my** 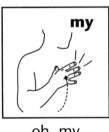	**Lord** 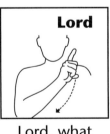	**what to do** 
Oh, my	Lord,	oh, my	Lord, what	shall I do?

① hand flat against chest

Grade 3, Teacher Edition, page 162

SIGNING 6 (CONTINUED)

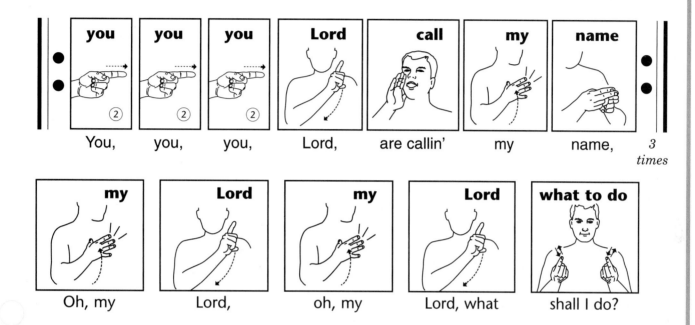

you	you	you	Lord	call	my	name
You,	you,	you,	Lord,	are callin'	my	name, *3 times*

my	Lord	my	Lord	what to do
Oh, my	Lord,	oh, my	Lord, what	shall I do?

② point up to heaven—denotes location of reference (Lord)

SIGNING 7

Peace Like a River

African American Spiritual

VERSE 1

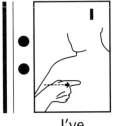 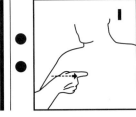 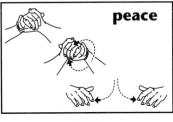 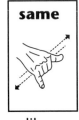 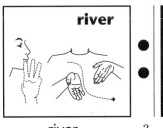

I	**have**	**peace**	**same**	**river**
I've	got	peace	like a	river,

3 times

VERSE 2

  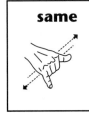 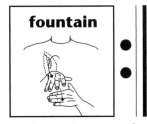

I	**have**	**joy**	**same**	**fountain**
I've	got	joy ①	like a	fountain,

3 times

VERSE 3

  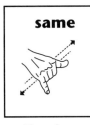 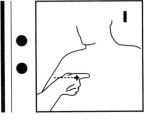 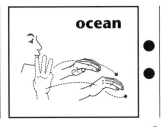

I	**have**	**love**	**same**	**ocean**
I've	got	love	like the	ocean,

3 times

ending for each verse

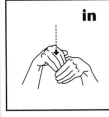 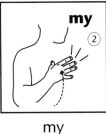 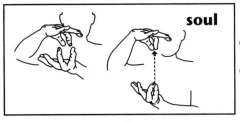

in	**my**	**soul**
in	my ②	soul.

① sometimes signed with both hands

② palm flat against chest

SIGNING **8**

You're a Grand Old Flag

*Words and Music by
George M. Cohan*

flag

You're a

wonderful

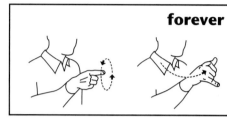

flag

grand old flag, you're a high-flying flag;

forever

And forever

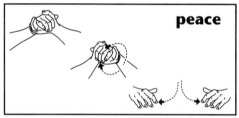

peace

in peace

continue

may you

flag

wave;

flag

You're the

represents

emblem of

land

the land

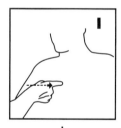

I

I

love

love,

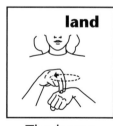

land

The home

of

of the

free

free and the

① *Flag* should be a small figure-8.
Wave should be a large figure-8.

SIGNING **8** (CONTINUED)

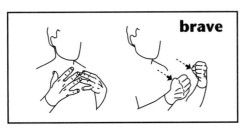

brave.

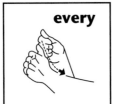

Ev'ry

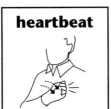

heart beats

true under

red, white, and blue,

Where there's

never a

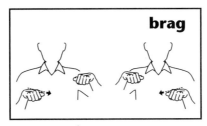

boast or

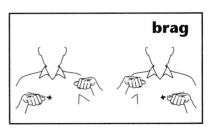

brag;

But should auld

acquaintance

be

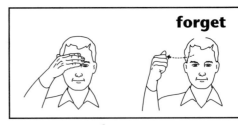

forgot,

① *Flag* should be a small figure-8.

SIGNING **8** (CONTINUED)

(gesture: two "V" hands, fingers pointed out, moving in circular motion away from body.)	wonderful 	flag 
Keep your eye on the	grand old	flag.

① *Flag* should be a small figure-8.

SIGNING 9

Pust' 'vsegda budet sonse (May the Sun Shine Forever)

Music by A. Ostrovsky

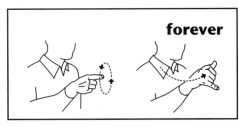

May the

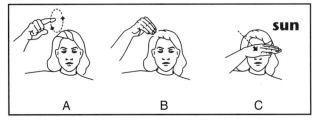

A   B   C

sun

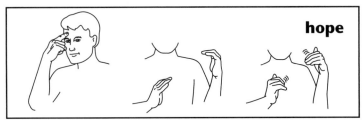

shine for-

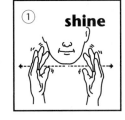

ever,

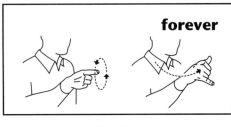

May blue

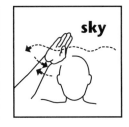

skies

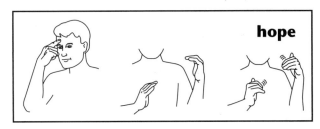

be for-

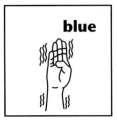

ever,

① sign above head—denotes location of object shining (sun)

SIGNING 9 (CONTINUED)

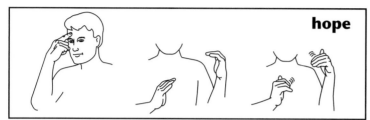

May there

ev-

er be

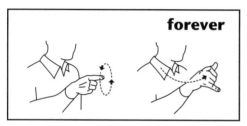

Mama,

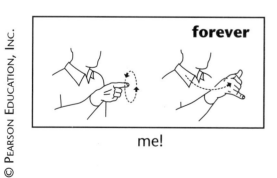

May there

ev-

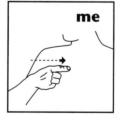

er be

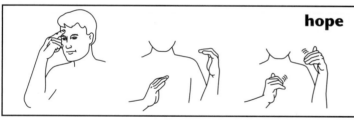

me!

SIGNING 10

Greetings

Words and Rhythmic Setting by Andrea Schafer

Polish	**hello**	**Polish**	**good**	**morning**
Cześć!	Hello!	*Dzień dobry!*	Good	morning!

Polish	**happy** ①	**meet**
Bardzo mimilo.	Pleased to	meet you.

① often signed with both hands

 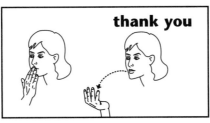 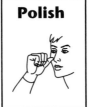 

Polish	**thank you**	**Polish**	**you're welcome**
Dzię Kuję.	Thank you.	*Proszę.*	You're welcome.

  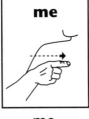   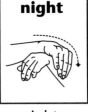

Polish	**excuse**	**me**	**Polish**	**good**	**night**
Przepraszam.	Excuse	me.	*Dobranoc.*	Good	night.

This is an excellent song to learn common greetings in sign language. Each sign should be made with the proper facial expression or nod of the head.

Two index fingers used in the sign for *meet* represents two people meeting each other.

SIGNING 11

El mes de abril (The Month of April)

Folk Song from Spain

spring

now

The month of April's   here,

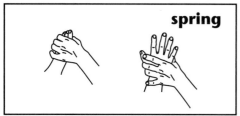
bird

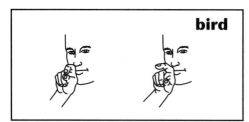
song

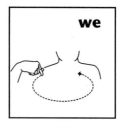
we

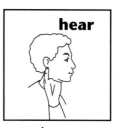
hear

The cuckoo's   song   we   hear.

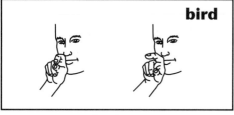
bird

song

Cuckoo,   cuckoo,

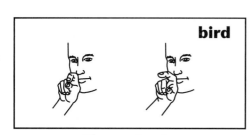
bird

song

we

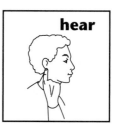
hear

The cuckoo's   song   we   hear.

SIGNING 12

Hevenu shalom aleichem
(We Come to Greet You in Peace)

Hebrew Folk Song

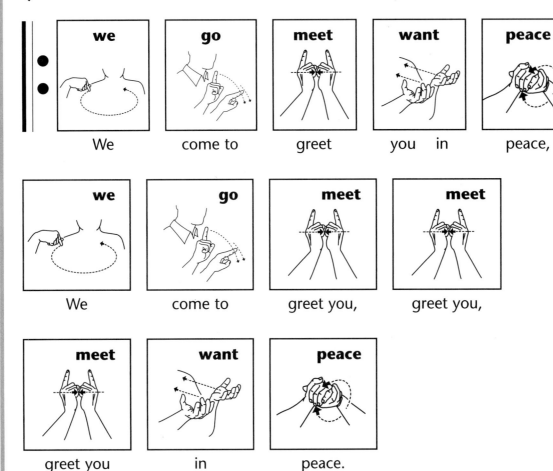

we	go	meet	want	peace
We	come to	greet	you in	peace,

repeat 3 times

we	go	meet	meet
We	come to	greet you,	greet you,

meet	want	peace
greet you	in	peace.

ASL is a language based on meaning; therefore, although the word *come* is used in the phrase *We come to greet you in peace,* the sign for *go* is used to indicate approaching another person.

The index finger is often used in ASL to indicate a person. The sign for *greet* is two index fingers or *persons* approaching each other.

Grade 3, Teacher Edition, page 378

SIGNING 13

Manual Alphabet

A B C D E F G

H I J K L M N

O P Q R S T U

V W X Y Z

SIGNING 14

Numbers

1   2   3

4   5   6

7   8   9

Note: Often signed with palm in for numbers 1–5 and palm out for numbers 6–9

10

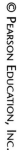

KEYBOARD

Table of Contents

KEYBOARD

KEYBOARD 1

One-line/Two-line Reading

Use black-key locators to determine the placement of the steps and skips on the keyboard.

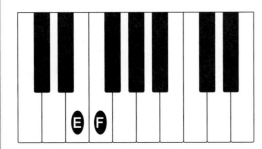

Step Up

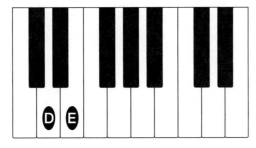

Skip Up

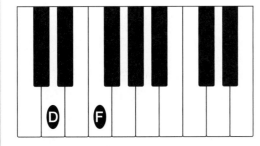

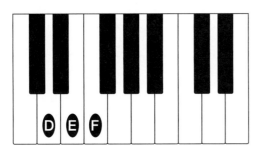
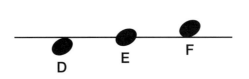

Grade 3, Teacher Edition, page 6

Keyboard 1 (continued)

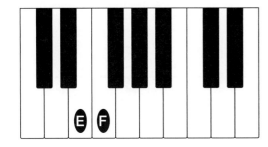

Step Down
F   E

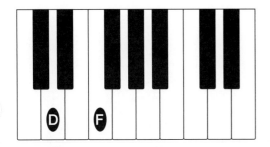

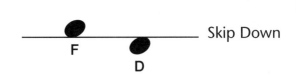
Skip Down
F   D

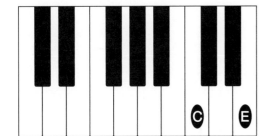

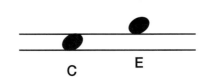
C   E

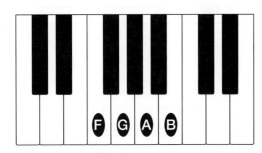

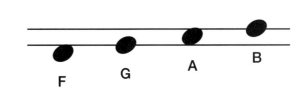
F   G   A   B

KEYBOARD

KEYBOARD 2

One-line/Two-line Fingering

Fingers, fingers, which fingers do I use?

Write the fingerings you choose in the boxes above the notes.

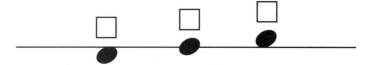

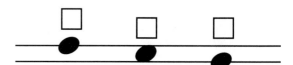

Grade 3, Teacher Edition, page 6

KEYBOARD 3

Beat and Key Recognition

Use the following speech piece to find high and low pitches.

Name, Name, What's Your Name?

Jim Solomon

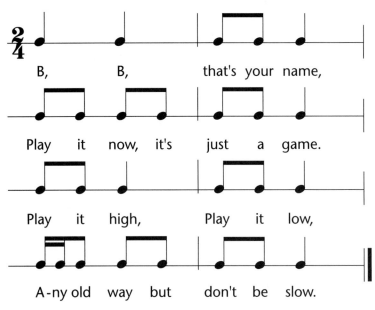

$\frac{2}{4}$

B, B, that's your name,

Play it now, it's just a game.

Play it high, Play it low,

A-ny old way but don't be slow.

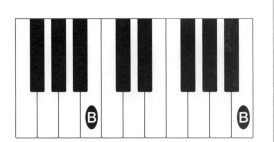

Student plays:

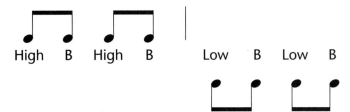

High B High B   Low B Low B

Now try the game with:

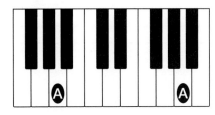

and

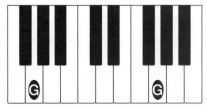

KEYBOARD 4

Five-line Reading and Fingering

Play these notes.

Skip Up

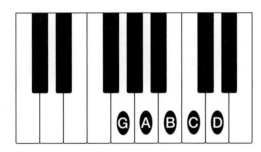

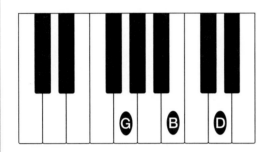

Step Up

Write the fingerings you choose in the boxes above the staff.

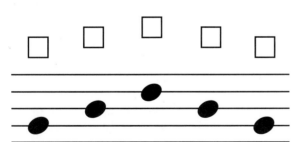

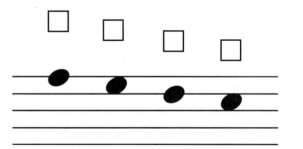

KEYBOARD 5

Five-line Reading of a Quarter Note Accompaniment

Gypsy in the Moonlight

Folk Song from Trinidad

Play these notes.

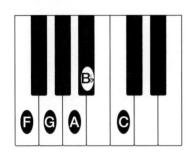

l. h.   **5 4 3 2   1**

Play with the left hand thumb on middle C.

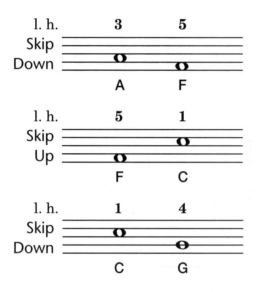

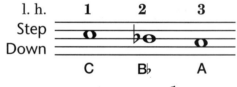

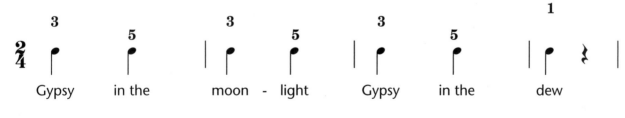

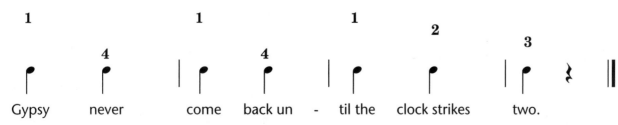

KEYBOARD 6

Same and Different Phrases

Au clair de la lune (In the Moonlight)

Traditional Song from France

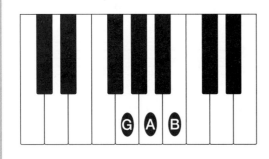

r. h.   **3**   **2**   **1**

r. h.   **1**   **2**   **3**

Play only the phrases that are the "same."

r.h.
```
                3           3
           2        2            2   2
   1   1   1                 1               1
   Au  clair de la | lu - ne,  | Mon a - mi Pier - | rot, |
```

r.h.
```
                3           3
           2        2            2   2
   1   1   1                 1               1
   Prê -  te moi ta | plu - me, | Pour é - crire un   | mot; |
```

(no third phrase)

r.h.
```
                3           3
           2        2            2   2
   1   1   1                 1               1
   Ou - vre-moi ta | por - te,  | Pour l'a - mour de | Dieu. |
```

KEYBOARD 7

Preparing Steps and Repeated Tones

Play the repeated phrase segment *John Ka-na-ka, na-ka* using steps and repeated notes.

John Kanaka

Sea Shanty from the United States

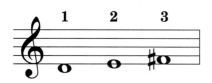

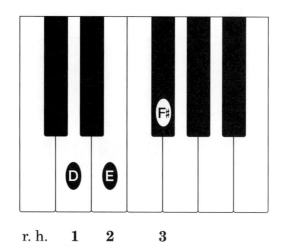

r. h.   1   2   3

KEYBOARD

KEYBOARD 8

Playing Melody

Play the *mi, re, do, la* pattern using fingers 5, 4, 3, and 1. Now play the melody for "*Hosisipa.*" Be aware of steps and repeated notes.

Hosisipa

Native American Game Song of the Sioux

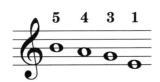

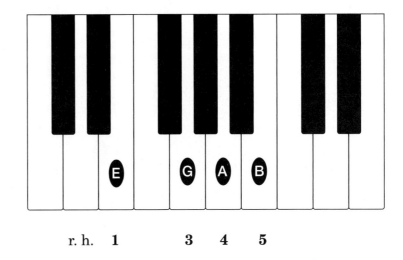

Grade 3, Teacher Edition, page 70

KEYBOARD 9

Playing a Song Using Sixteenth Notes

How many different patterns are there in "Love Somebody"? Use your right hand to play the patterns below.

Love Somebody (piano version)

Folk Song from the United States

#1)

		5	5				4
3					3		
			2				
1							
Love	some - bod -	y, |	yes,	I	do, |

#2)

		5	5			
3			4		3	
						2
1						
Love	some - bod -	y, |	yes,	I	do, |

#3)

3	3				3
	2 2 2 2				
		1		1	
Love	some - bod-y, but I |	won't	tell	who! |

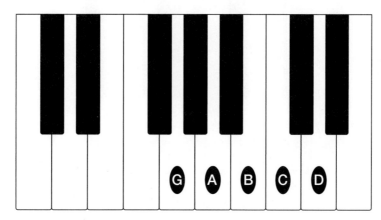

KEYBOARD 10

Playing an Ostinato Accompaniment

This ostinato accompaniment uses two alternating patterns. How will the last measure end?

Tender Shepherd

Music by Mark Charlap

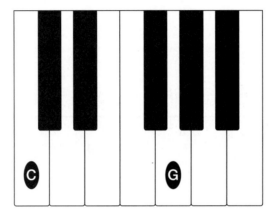

First Position

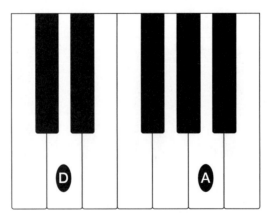

Second Position

Grade 3, Teacher Edition, page 116

KEYBOARD 11

Playing an Accompaniment

The accompaniment for *"Kum bachur atzel"* uses only two positions—a "C" position and a "G" position. Each position uses a *grace note*. To play a grace note, play the first note in the right hand and quickly play the second right-hand note, holding down only the key for the second note. Try this several times with the right hand until it is comfortable. Now add the left-hand note, making sure that the left-hand note sounds at the same time as the second right-hand note. Notice that the same accompaniment pattern is played a total of six times.

Kum bachur atzel (Hear the Rooster Crowing)   *Folk Song from Israel*

Use right-hand fingers 2 and 3 to play the grace note and the note that follows.

Play the right-hand pitches one at a time but connected, holding only the second key. The left-hand finger 2 plays the pitches with "down" stems.

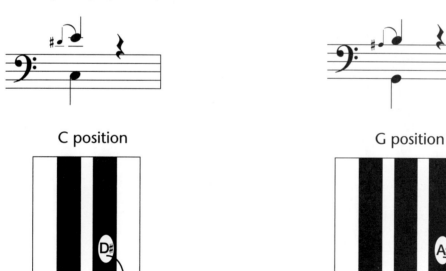

Hear the roos – ter | crow – ing, A - | crow – ing at the | dawn; |

KEYBOARD 12

Playing a Phrase Divided Between the Hands

Discover how many times the words "Hop Up, My Ladies" are found in the song. Each time you hear these words, play the phrase with two hands.

Hop Up, My Ladies

Folk Song from the United States

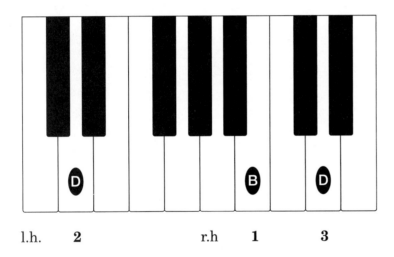

l.h. **2**   r.h **1**   **3**

r.h.   **3**   **3**   **3**

l.h. **2**

Hop up,   my | la - dies, |

KEYBOARD 13

Accompanying in Meter in 3 and in 2

Notice how the accompaniment changes in "Coffee Grows on White Oak Trees" when the meter changes from meter in 3 to meter in 2. Then, discuss an appropriate fingering before playing the accompaniment.

Coffee Grows on White Oak Trees

Folk Song from the United States

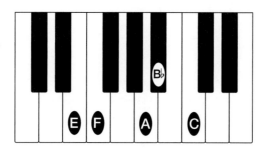

KEYBOARD 14

Playing an Ostinato Accompaniment

An ostinato is a short, repeated pattern. Use two measures of the pattern below for an introduction to the song "Good Morning."

Good Morning

Words and Music by Elizabeth Gilpatrick

INTRODUCTION

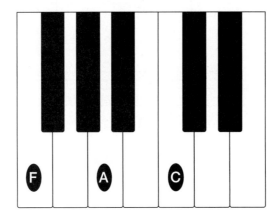

Grade 3, Teacher Edition, page 192

KEYBOARD 15

Playing in an Ensemble

Choose a partner and play the parts together.

Hot Cross Buns (Version 1)

Folk Song from England

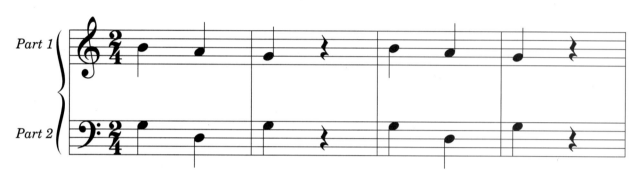

Play through again and change parts.

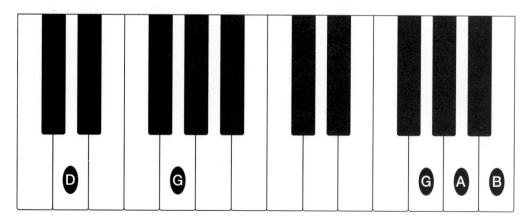

© PEARSON EDUCATION, INC.

KEYBOARD 16

Playing an Accompaniment

Practice the exercises below. When you feel comfortable with both exercises, play the accompaniment.

He's Got the Whole World in His Hands

African American Spiritual

Exercise 1

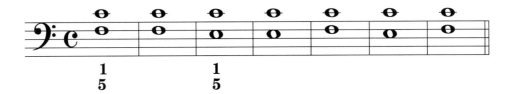

1
5   1
             5

Exercise 2

1   1
3   2
5   5

Accompaniment

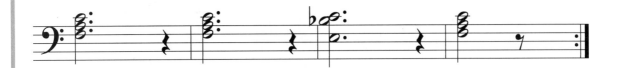

KEYBOARD 17

Timbre—Two-Part Accompaniment

Choose Part 1 or Part 2 to play as an accompaniment for "Peace Like a River."

Peace Like a River

African American Spiritual

| Part 1 A | E♭ | D | B♭ |
| Part 2 F | F | B♭ | C |

| A | B♮ | B♭ | B♭ |
| F | G | C | C |

| A | E♭ | D | B♭ |
| F | F | B♭ | C |

| A | | A | B♭ | A |
| F | | F | C | F |

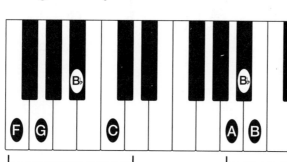

Part 2   Part 1

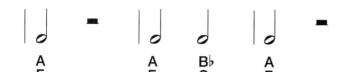

KEYBOARD 18

Harmony

Play this alternating-hand accompaniment using C-G and G-D.

Nani wale na hala (Lovely Hala Trees)

Folk Song from Hawaii

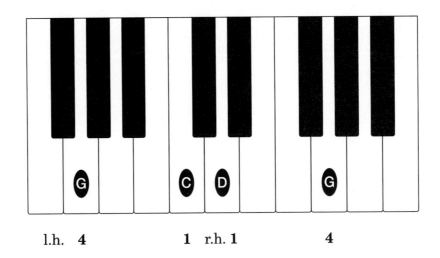

Grade 3, Teacher Edition, page 260

KEYBOARD 19

Playing a Phrase

Play these notes with the last phrase of *"Sarika keo."*

Sarika keo (Bird Song)

Folk Song from Cambodia

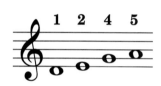

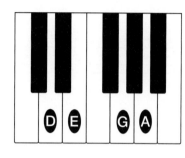

r.h.   1   2   4   5

KEYBOARD 20

Play a Song Part

Compare the staff notation to the keyboard diagram.

Wichita Hand Game Song 2

Game Song of the Wichita

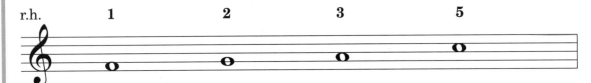

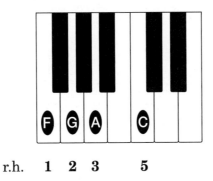

KEYBOARD 21

Playing a Two-Shape Accompaniment

Compare the staff notation to the keyboard diagram.

Al citrón

Latino Nonsense Song from California

l.h.   **1**
      2

l.h.   **1**
      3

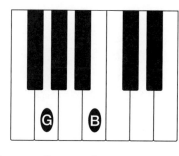

l.h.   **2**   **1**

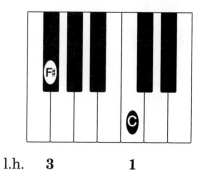

l.h.   **3**   **1**

KEYBOARD

Keyboard 22

Identifying and Playing Repeated Phrases

Listen closely as your teacher plays the melody line for the verse to "Big Beautiful Planet." Now sing along as your teacher plays the melody once again. There are four phrases in the verse. Which two are exactly alike? Play those two phrases using right-hand fingers 1, 2, and 3.

Big Beautiful Planet

Words and Music by Raffi

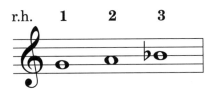

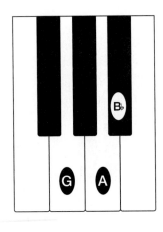

r.h.   1   2 3

KEYBOARD 23

Playing a Refrain

The refrain of "The World We Love" uses the pitches from middle C to the C above. Follow the directions to split the melody between the left hand and the right hand as you play the refrain.

The World We Love

Words and Music by Raffi and Michael Creber

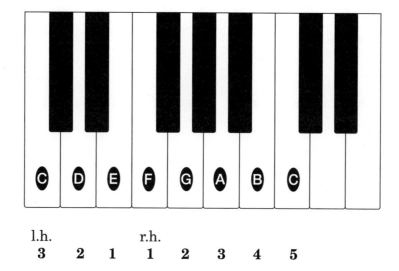

l.h.   r.h.
3   2   1   1   2   3   4   5

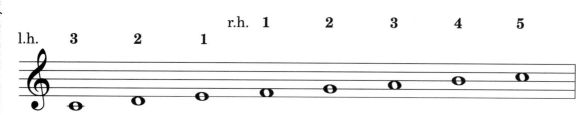

KEYBOARD

KEYBOARD **24**

Playing a Melody with an Octave Range

The World We Love

Words and Music by Raffi and Michael Creber

Look at the verse for "The World We Love." The lowest pitch is middle C and the highest pitch is the C above. Play the verse using both right hand and left hand.

Notice the first and third lines of the verse. What is the same? What is different?

On what finger does line 2 begin?
On what finger does line 4 begin?

Which hand will play on the words *brand new day*?

Challenge: Study the pitches used for the refrain. Determine how to play the refrain.

Grade 3, Teacher Edition, page 342

KEYBOARD 25

Playing an Accompaniment Ostinato

Remember that an ostinato is a short, repeated pattern. Study the two positions used in the ostinato below.

Knock No More!

Words and Music by Elizabeth Kilpatrick

Position 1

Position 2

Play the ostinato using left-hand fingers 5, 3, and 1.

Now play the accompaniment.

KEYBOARD

KEYBOARD 26

Playing a Melody with Shifting Fingerings

Look at the phrases of "Chrismus a Come." How are they similar?

The same fingering may be used for each of the phrases. Move your hand so that finger 3 begins each phrase. Practice each phrase carefully before playing the entire melody.

Chrismus a Come

Folk Song from Jamaica

Phrase One

Phrase Two

Phrase Three

Phrase Four

Grade 3, Teacher Edition, page 396

RECORDER

Table of Contents

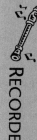

RECORDER

RECORDER 1

Playing G and A

This recorder part will give you additional practice playing G and A. Remember to whisper *daah* in the style of the music.

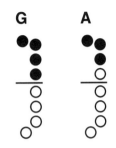

Hello to All the Children of the World

Words by Nancy Klein
Music by Nancy Klein and Pam Beall

REFRAIN

Fine

VERSE

D.C. al Fine

RECORDER 2

Playing A and B

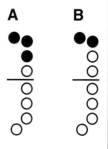

This recorder part will give you additional practice playing A and B. Remember to tongue repeated pitches clearly.

Ambos a dos (Go Two by Two)

Folk Song from Latin America

REFRAIN

VERSE

RECORDER

RECORDER 3

Playing G and A

This recorder part will give you additional practice playing G and A. Play the countermelody as others sing the song.

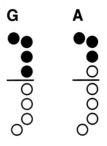

Joy to the World

Words and Music by Hoyt Axton

RECORDER 4

More Practice Playing A and B

Look at the two recorder parts below. Which one uses syncopation? First practice the melody that does not use syncopation.

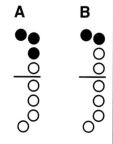

A   B

Ahora voy a cantarles (Now Hear the Song)

Folk Song from Argentina

Part 1

Part 2

RECORDER

RECORDER 5

Playing a "BAG" Song

Read the countermelody below. Notice it sometimes has the same melody as the song. As you play, make sure you cover the holes on your recorder securely.

G   A   B

Great Day

African American Spiritual

REFRAIN

Fine

VERSE

D.C. al Fine

Grade 3, Teacher Edition, page 58

RECORDER 6

Making Choices

Look at the two countermelodies below. Are they the same or different? Play both of these countermelodies. Choose the one you would like to play as others sing the original folk melody.

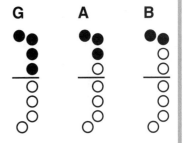

G   A   B

Love Somebody

Folk Song from the United States

Countermelody 1

Countermelody 2

RECORDER

RECORDER 7

Playing G and A

Play the countermelody below to accompany "Old Dan Tucker." Notice that it uses only G and A. Whisper *daah* in the style of the music as you play.

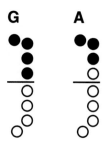

Old Dan Tucker

Folk Song from the United States

VERSE

REFRAIN

Grade 3, Teacher Edition, page 96

RECORDER **8**

Mixing Countermelodies

When you are comfortable playing both of the countermelodies below, combine them in different ways. For example, play phrase one of countermelody 1 followed by phrase two of countermelody 2.

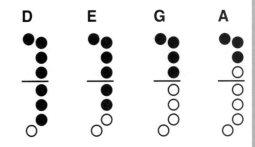

Tender Shepherd

Music by Mark Charlap

Countermelody 1

Countermelody 2

RECORDER

RECORDER 9

Playing "BAG"

Feel the beats grouped in sets of three as you play this countermelody to accompany "The Juniper Tree." When playing leaps between G and B, make sure you move your fingers together.

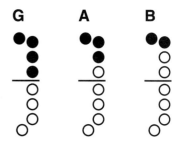

G A B

The Juniper Tree

Folk Song from Arkansas

RECORDER 10

Playing with Style

Whisper *daah* in the style of the music as you play this countermelody. Carefully observe the quarter rests. Remember that each quarter rest equals one beat of silence.

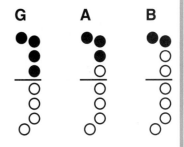

Hop Up, My Ladies

Folk Song from the United States

"Hop Up, My Ladies" Collected, adapted and arranged by John A. Lomax and Alan Lomax. TRO © Copyright 1941 (Renewed) Ludlow Music, Inc., New York, NY. Used by permission.

RECORDER

RECORDER 11

Playing Low D and E

Review the fingering for low D and E on your recorder. Remember to whisper *daah* gently when playing notes in the lower register. When you can finger these new notes, play the countermelody below while others sing "Do, Lord."

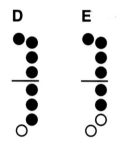

Do, Lord

African American Spiritual

RECORDER 12

Changing Meter

Look at the recorder part written below. Notice that it uses the notes G and A. The first part of this song is written in $\frac{3}{4}$ and the second part is written in $\frac{2}{4}$. As you play, accent the first beat of each measure in order to feel the changing meter.

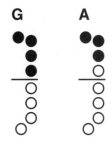

Coffee Grows on White Oak Trees

Folk Song from the United States

RECORDER

RECORDER 13

Feeling Meter in 3

The countermelody below uses the notes D and E. As you play, feel the beats grouped in sets of three. Tongue each note.

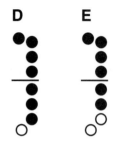

Pretty Saro

Folk Song from the United States

Grade 3, Teacher Edition, page 216

RECORDER **14**

Chord Changes

How many different chords are needed to
accompany this song? How many different notes
will you play on your recorder?

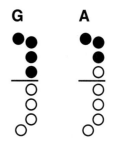

He's Got the Whole World in His Hands

African American Spiritual

RECORDER 15

Playing Another "BAG" Song

Play this recorder part while others sing Section A of the song. Take a breath after each breath mark (**,**) and at each rest.

G **A** **B**

I've Been Working on the Railroad

Work Song from the United States

A

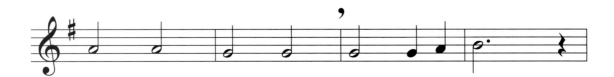

Grade 3, Teacher Edition, page 242

RECORDER 16

Meter in 3 with G, A, and B

As you play this recorder part, feel the steady
beat moving in sets of three. Be sure to fill
each long note with sound.

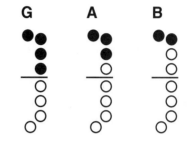

Take Me Out to the Ball Game

Words by Jack Norworth
Music by Albert von Tilzer

RECORDER 17

Meter in 2 with G and A

As you play this recorder part, feel the beats grouped in sets of two. Remember to tongue notes of the same pitch clearly and observe all the rests.

G   A

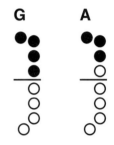

You're a Grand Old Flag

Words and Music by George M. Cohan

Grade 3, Teacher Edition, page 264

RECORDER 18

Adding Low E

Review the fingerings for G, A, and low E before reading the part below. Practice playing leaps between G and low E, remembering to move your fingers together. When you play the recorder part below, observe all the rests.

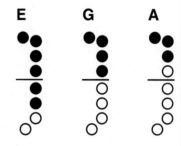

Children's Song from Panama

Al tambor (The Drum Song)

RECORDER

RECORDER 19

Feeling Duple Meter

When you know the fingerings for G, A, B, low D, and low E, play the countermelody below on your recorder. Feel the beat as you play. Remember to cover the holes securely and move fingers together when playing leaps.

D   E   G   A   B

Bonavist' Harbour

Folk Song from Newfoundland

VERSE

REFRAIN

Grade 3, Teacher Edition, page 294

RECORDER 20

A Calypso Countermelody

Play this countermelody on your recorder as others sing this folk song. Feel the quarter note pulse as you whisper *daah* in the style of the music.

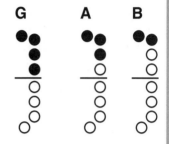

G   A   B

Four White Horses

Folk Song from the Caribbean

RECORDER

RECORDER 21

Feeling Beats in 3

Play the countermelody below on your recorder as others sing and dance. Feel the beats grouped in sets of three. Remember to observe all the rests.

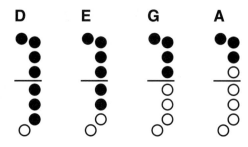

D   E   G   A

Nie chcę cię znác (Don't Want to Know You)   *Folk Song from Poland*

RECORDER 22

Feeling Meter in 3

As you play the countermelody below, feel the meter in 3. When playing low D and E, whisper *daah* gently. You need very little air to play a good sound on these low notes.

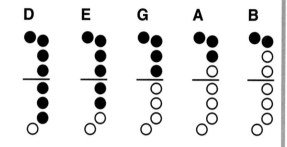

El sapito (The Little Toad)

Music by Wilbur Alpírez Quesada

RECORDER

RECORDER 23

Another "BAG" Song

As you play this countermelody, carefully observe the quarter rests. Notice that you need to rest on the first beat of each two-measure phrase during the first part of the song. Feel one beat of silence on each rest.

G   A   B

It's a Beautiful Day

Words and Music by Greg Scelsa

RECORDER **24**

More Practice with Low D and E

Playing notes in the low register of the recorder
can be difficult. Remember to use very little air
and cover the holes firmly with your fingers. Play
the countermelody below to accompany this
popular Mexican folk song.

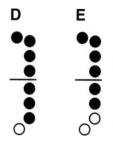

Don Gato

Folk Song from Mexico

RECORDER

RECORDER 25

Playing with Style

Feel the beats grouped in sets of two as you play this countermelody to accompany the rock 'n' roll song, "Rockin' Robin." In order to break the sound between notes of the same pitch, whisper *daah* on each note. Think the words *long* (for half notes) and *short* (for quarter notes) as you play the rhythm.

G **A**

Rockin' Robin

Words and Music by Leon René

RECORDER 26

Melodic Phrases

Look at the countermelody below and compare the four phrases. Notice that some phrases are the same while others are different. How is the last phrase different from the third phrase?

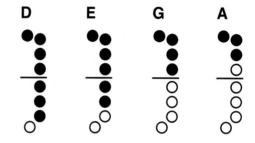

Hanuka, Hanuka

Words and Music by Flory Jagoda

VERSE

REFRAIN

RECORDER

RECORDER 27

Soprano Recorder Fingerings

Practice fingering each note from lowest to highest.

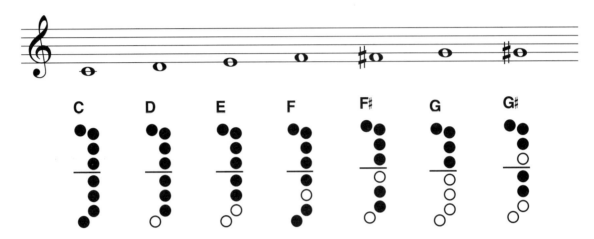

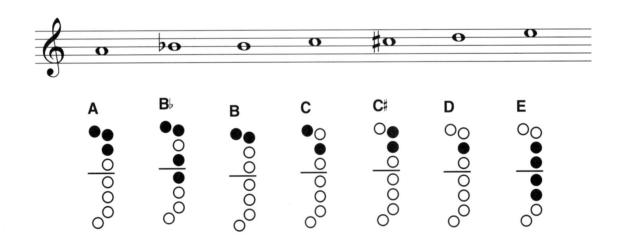

ACTIVITY MASTERS

Table of Contents

© PEARSON EDUCATION, INC.

ACTIVITY MASTER 1

A Letter to Home

This year, your child will be participating in a music class designed to foster lifelong appreciation of music through active music making. The sequenced music instruction will help your child develop musical skills and understanding, using music of various styles from the United States and around the world. In addition to developing specific musical skills, your child's studies in other areas will be enhanced by instruction that links concepts across the curriculum.

Your child will also have opportunities to participate in theme-based music making. Some possible themes include American music, world music, friends, families, self-esteem, animals, ecology, storytelling, choral singing, seasons, and celebrations. Your child may also be involved in classroom and/or school-wide performances, and you will be invited to attend or volunteer to assist with these performances.

You can also reinforce your child's music learning at home. Consider listening to music together and talking about it. Ask your child to share songs learned in music class. Attend local concerts to help foster appropriate audience behavior. These experiences will help make music meaningful at school, at home, and in the community.

Sincerely,

ACTIVITY MASTER 2

Una Carta al Hogar

Este año, su niño(a) tomará parte en una clase de música que le ayudará a adquirir una apreciación de música durante toda la vida mediante su participación en actividades musicales. La instrucción de música, que está estructurada en una secuencia lógica, le ayudará a su niño(a) a desarrollar destrezas y conocimientos musicales, al experimentar distintos estilos de música de los Estados Unidos y de todas partes del mundo. Además del desarrollo de destrezas musicales, su niño(a) mejorará en los otros campos de estudio porque la instrucción relaciona conceptos provenientes de todo el plan de estudios.

Su niño(a) también tendrá oportunidades de tomar parte en actividades musicales basadas en un tema. Entre estos temas hay música americana, música mundial, amigos, familias, auto-estima, animales, ecología, cuentos, canto coral, estaciones y celebraciones. Tal vez su niño(a) pueda estar envuelto en actuaciones en la clase y/o para toda la escuela, y se le invitará a usted(es) a asistir o a ayudar con estas actuaciones como voluntario(a). Usted(es) también puede(n) reforzar en casa el aprendizaje de música de su niño(a). Consideren escuchar a música juntos y después hablar sobre lo que oyeron. Pídale a su niño(a) que comparta con usted(es) las canciones que ha aprendido en la clase de música. Llévelo(la) a conciertos de la zona para ayudarle a experimentar en la audiencia conducta apropriada. Todo esto ayudará a hacer que la música sea una experiencia significativa para su niño(a) en la escuela, en casa y en la comunidad.

Sinceramente,

ACTIVITY MASTER 3

Dynamics in a Flash

Use the flash cards below to show changes in dynamics.

p	*f*
mp	*mf*

ACTIVITY MASTER 4

Up, Down, or Same?

Circle the word that shows the direction of the melody.

1. Upward   Downward   Same

2. Upward   Downward   Same

3. Upward   Downward   Same

4. Upward   Downward   Same

5. Upward   Downward   Same

6. Upward   Downward   Same

ACTIVITY MASTER 5

Timbre Journal

Keep a journal of the timbres you hear each day. List who or what you heard by writing the name of the person or thing that made each sound in the chart below.

	Monday	Tuesday	Wednesday	Thursday	Friday
Male					
Female					
Child					
Animal					
Group					
Machine					

Grade 3, Teacher Edition, page 32

ACTIVITIES

ACTIVITY MASTER 6

What Kind of Rhythm?

Look at the rhythm patterns shown below and decide if each pattern is syncopated or a steady beat. Circle your answers.

1.    syncopated   steady beat

2.    syncopated   steady beat

3.    syncopated   steady beat

4.    syncopated   steady beat

5. 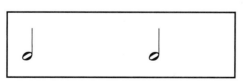   syncopated   steady beat

ACTIVITY MASTER 7

Smooth or Separated?

Decide which sounds are *staccato* and which sounds are *legato*. Circle your answers.

1.

staccato   *legato*

2.

staccato   *legato*

3.

staccato   *legato*

4.

staccato   *legato*

5.

staccato   *legato*

6.

staccato   *legato*

ACTIVITY MASTER 8
Crossword Puzzle 1

<u>Vocabulary List</u>
accompaniment
beat
cello
dynamics
forte
la
ostinato
pentatonic
phrase
piano
pizzicato
rhythm
slow
syncopation
tempo
tie
timbre
underground
verse

Across	Down
1. The part of a song where the melody stays the same even when the lyrics change (p. 97)	**2.** A rhythm where the note that is stressed comes between two beats (p. 55)
7. Songs that have only five pitches (p. 30)	**3.** Many African American spirituals were used to send messages in the _____ Railroad (p. 48)
10. A repeated rhythm or melody pattern (p. 41)	**4.** The pitch that is a step lower than *low ___* is called *low so* (p. 69)
11. A part that supports a main melody (p. 36)	**5.** Loud (p. 7)
16. The speed of the beat (p. 50)	**6.** Plucked (p. 113)
17. Yo-Yo Ma plays this instrument (p. 38)	**7.** A musical sentence (p. 20)
18. The regular pulse felt in most music (p. 10)	**8.** The louds and softs in music (p. 6)
	9. A pattern of long and short sounds and silences (p. 10)
	12. Soft (p. 7)
	13. The special sound each voice or instrument makes (p. 73)
	14. *Adagio* (p. 50)
	15. A musical symbol that joins two notes together to create a longer rhythm (p. 53)

Name _____   Class _____

ACTIVITY MASTER 9

Fill-in-the-Blanks

Fill in the missing words. Choose from this list.

  adagio   tempo

  allegro   moderato

  subito

Bill sat down on the couch in his living room to listen to his favorite CD. The first

song he heard was quite slow. As he thought about the speed of the beat, or the

① _____, he decided that it was ② _____ because the

music was slow.

The next song was fast. Bill jumped up and started to dance. If he had been reading

the music, it might have been marked ③ _____.

Soon Bill heard music coming from the street. He looked out the window and saw

the school marching band. Since the music was not too fast and not too slow, he

decided that the tempo was ④ _____.

When he opened the window so that he could hear better, the music suddenly

became very loud. He remembered that in school that day he learned another

word for suddenly: ⑤ _____.

ACTIVITY MASTER 10

Family Ties

Each instrument below belongs to one of the four families of instruments.

S = Strings   P = Percussion   W = Woodwinds   B = Brass

Write the correct letter in the space provided for each instrument.

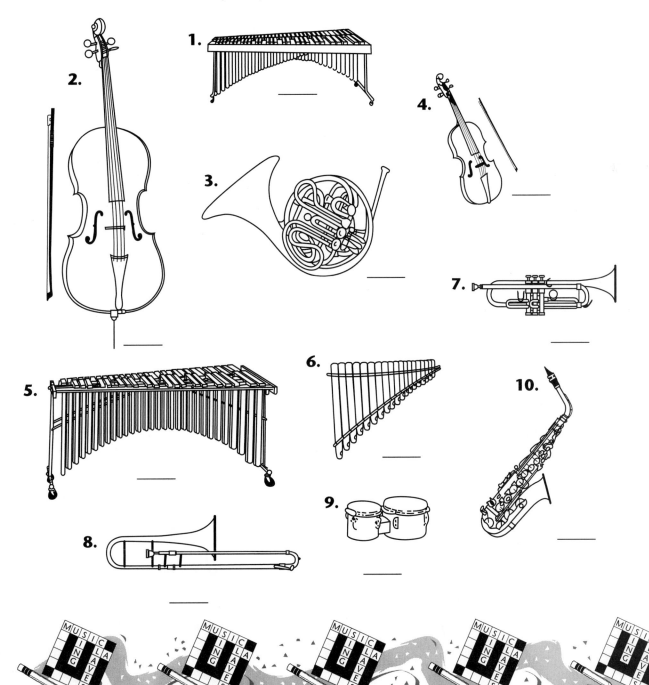

ACTIVITY MASTER 11

Meter-Made

Decide which rhythm patterns belong in $\frac{2}{4}$, $\frac{3}{4}$, and $\frac{4}{4}$ meter. Write the correct meters before each pattern. The first one has been done for you.

1.

2.

3.

4.

5.

6.

7.

8.

Grade 3, Teacher Edition, page 204

ACTIVITY MASTER 12

Crossword Puzzle 2

<u>Vocabulary List</u>

accent
Bernstein
canon
coda
crescendo
Ennanga
flute
introduction
kayagum
mallets
measure
octave
proverb
scat
subito
tonal
upbeat
xylophone

Across	Down
5. The musical sign that tells you to get louder (p. 200)	**1.** Gives emphasis to a single tone or chord (p. 209)
7. This composer's first name is Elmer (p. 145)	**2.** The space between two bar lines (p. 131)
9. Music that ends a song after the words are sung (p. 138)	**3.** In music it is played before the words are sung (p. 138)
10. The home tone of a song is also called the _____ center (p. 215)	**4.** One or more notes before the first strong beat of a phrase (p. 133)
12. The distance between one note and the next higher or lower note that has the same name (p. 143)	**6.** An instrumental piece by William Grant Still (p. 127)
	8. One of the oldest known instruments (p. 184)
	11. Sticks with rubber, felt, wood, or yarn balls on one end (p. 148)
16. Means "wood sound" (p. 148)	**13.** A Korean folk instrument (p. 137)
17. A form of jazz singing (p. 158)	**14.** A short, true saying that's easy to understand (p. 224)
18. Sudden (p. 125)	**15.** A follow-the-leader musical process in which all perform the same pattern, but start at different times (p. 190)

ACTIVITY MASTER 13

Identifying Form

Look at the illustrations below and identify the form they represent. Choose from AB, ABA, AABA, and AAAB. Write your answers in the spaces provided.

1.

_____ _____ _____

2.

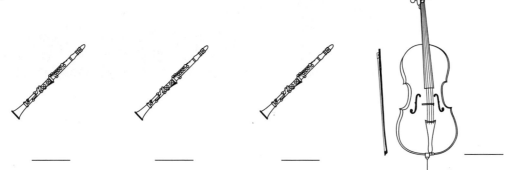

_____ _____ _____ _____

3.

_____ _____

4.

_____ _____ _____ _____

ACTIVITY MASTER 14

Strong and Weak Beats

Identify all the strong and weak beats in the rhythm patterns below. Mark all strong beats with an *S* and all weak beats with a *W*.

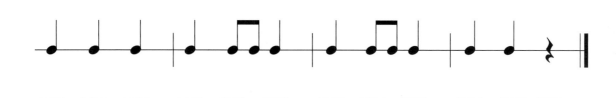

ACTIVITY MASTER 15

The Legend of the Bluebonnet

Once, long ago in the land of the Comanche, there was a great drought and famine and pestilence. The dancers danced to the sound of the drums and prayed for rain. They watched and waited for the healing rains, and danced again. No rains came.

Among the children of the tribe there was a small girl named She-Who-Is-Alone. She watched the dancers and held her warrior doll. Her doll wore beaded leggings and a headdress of brilliant blue feathers from the bird that cries "Jay-Jay." She loved this doll very much. Her doll was the only thing she had left from the happy days before the great famine took her parents and grandparents from her.

As She-Who-is-Alone sat and held her doll, the Shaman, or Wise Man, came to speak to the people. He told them that the Great Spirits were unhappy. He said that the people had been selfish, taking every thing from the earth, giving nothing in return. He said that the people must make a sacrifice and must make a burnt offering of their most prized possession. The Shaman said the ashes of this offering should be scattered to the home of the Four Winds—North, South, East, and West. When this sacrifice was made the drought would cease. Life would be restored to the land.

The people talked among themselves. The warriors were sure it was not their bow that the Great Spirits wanted. The women knew that this was not their special blanket. She-Who-Is-Alone looked at her doll, her most valued possession. She knew what the Great Spirits wanted and knew what she must do.

While everyone slept she took her warrior doll and one stick that burned from the teepee fire and made her way to the hill where the Shaman had spoken—"Oh Great Spirits," she called out, "here is my warrior doll, the only thing I have left from happy days with my family. It is my most valued possession. Please accept it."

Then she made a fire and thrust her precious doll into it. When the flames died down, she scooped up a handful of ashes and scattered them to the four winds—North, South, East, and West. Then, her cheeks wet with tears, she lie down and fell asleep.

The first light of morning woke her and she looked out over the hills. Stretching from all sides where the ashes had fallen, the ground was covered with flowers, beautiful blue flowers, as blue as the feathers in the hair of her beloved doll.

Now every spring the Great Spirits remember the sacrifice of a very small girl and fill the hills and valleys of the land now called Texas with beautiful blue flowers. And this is so to this very day.

ACTIVITY MASTER 16

Adding Quarter Rests

Practice making quarter rests by tracing the dotted-line rests below. Begin each rest at the top and work down.

Now notate the missing quarter rests in the rhythm pattern below.

ACTIVITY MASTER 17

Composing Rhythm Ostinatos

Each of the three rhythm patterns below needs another measure. Add your own pattern to the last measure of each exercise. Perform your ostinatos for the class.

1.

2.

3.

Grade 3, Teacher Edition, page 354

ACTIVITY MASTER 18

Keyboard Diagram

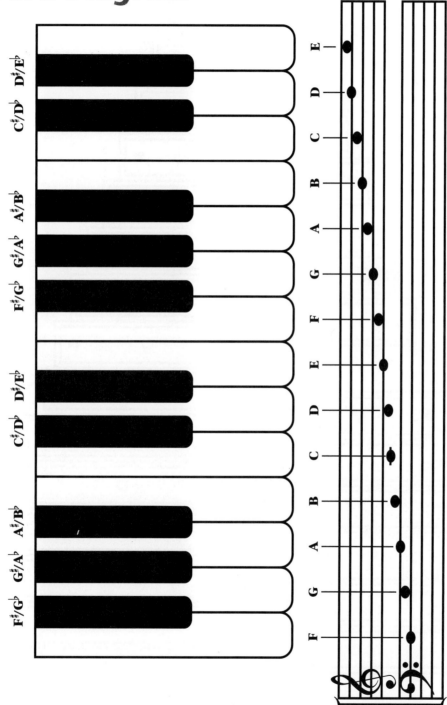

ACTIVITY MASTER 19

Bell Diagram

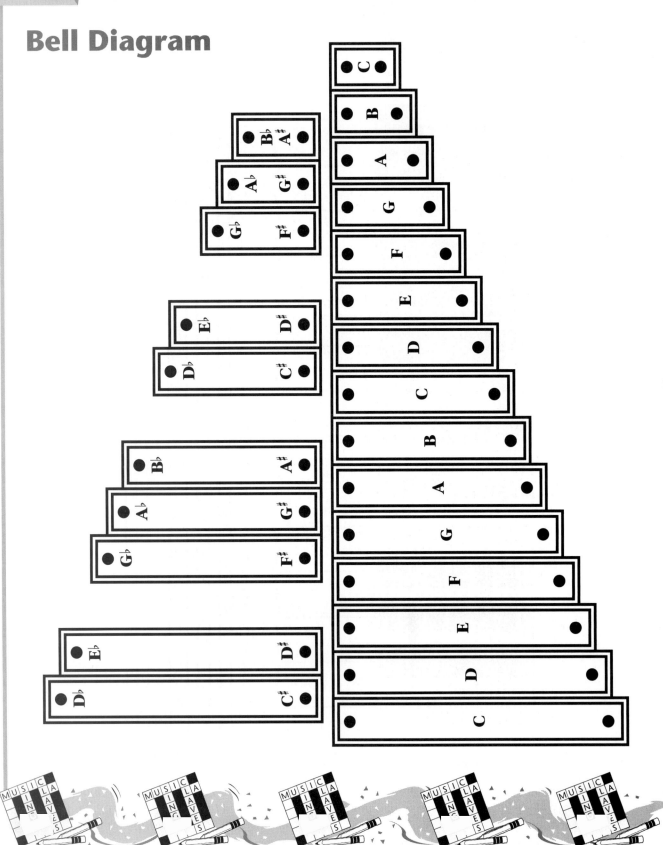

Name _____   Class _____

ACTIVITY MASTER 20

Autoharp Diagram

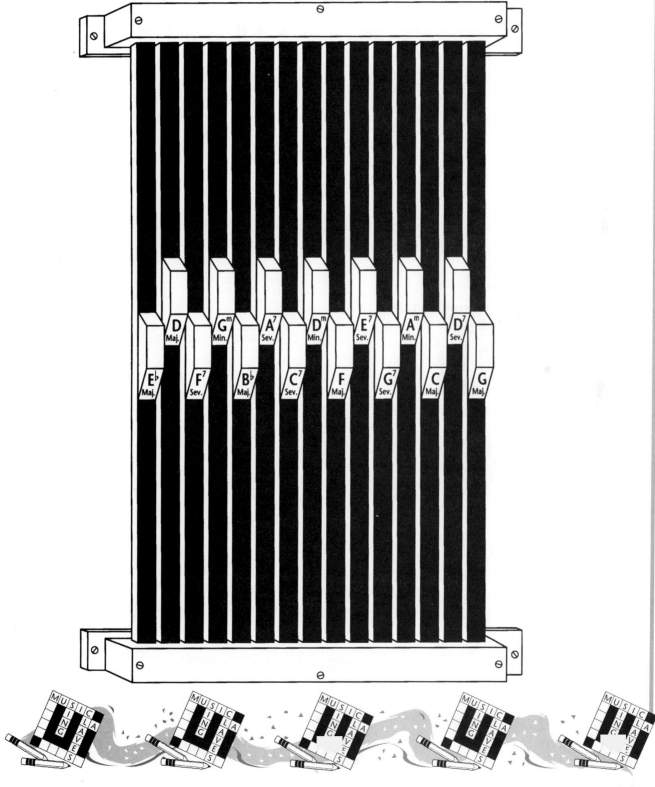

© PEARSON EDUCATION, INC.

J-21

ACTIVITY MASTERS ANSWER KEY

J-5   Activity Master 4: Up, Down, or Same?

1. Upward

2. Downward

3. Same

4. Downward

5. Same

6. Upward

J-7   Activity Master 6: What Kind of Rhythm?

1. steady beat

2. syncopated

3. syncopated

4. steady beat

5. steady beat

J-8   Activity Master 7: Smooth or Separated?

1. *staccato*

2. *legato*

3. *staccato*

4. *legato*

5. *staccato*

6. *legato*

J-9   Activity Master 8: Crossword Puzzle 1

ACTIVITY MASTERS ANSWER KEY (CONTINUED)

J-10 Activity Master 9: Fill-in-the-Blanks

1. *tempo*
2. *adagio*
3. *allegro*
4. *moderato*
5. *subito*

J-11 Activity Master 10: Family Ties

1. Percussion
2. Strings
3. Brass
4. Strings
5. Percussion
6. Woodwinds
7. Brass
8. Brass
9. Percussion
10. Woodwinds

J-12 Activity Master 11: Meter-Made

1. Answer provided on page.
2. $\frac{3}{4}$
3. $\frac{4}{4}$
4. $\frac{3}{4}$
5. $\frac{4}{4}$
6. $\frac{4}{4}$
7. $\frac{2}{4}$
8. $\frac{3}{4}$

J-13 Activity Master 12: Crossword Puzzle 2

J-14 Activity Master 13: Identifying Form

1. ABA
2. AAAB
3. AB
4. AABA

J-15 Activity Master 14: Strong and Weak Beats

S-W-W | S-W-W | S-W-W | S-W-W | S-W-W | S-W-W | S-W-W | S-W-W|

Teacher Notes

Art Credits

Assessment
B-17, Dan Grant.

Reading
D-2, Reggie Holladay; D-3, Donna Catanese; D-6, Reggie Holladay; D-7, Reggie Holladay; D-8, Burgandy Beam; D-10, Burgandy Beam; D-14, Burgandy Beam; D-17, Donna Catanese; D-23 , Burgandy Beam.

Activity Master
J-8, Laura Freeman; J-11, Burgandy Beam; J-14, Burgandy Beam.

Orff icons
All art Tony Nuccio.

Signing
All art Burgandy Beam.

Acknowledgments

Credit and appreciation are due publishers and copyright owners for use of the following:
A-4: "La pulga de San José" © 1994 José-Luis Orozco, Spanish lyrics and English lyrics and musical arrangement. All Rights Reserved. **A-6:** "Ahora voy a cantarles" (Now Hear the Song I'll Sing You), from Folk Songs of the Americas, 1965, by Albert Lancaster Lloyd. Copyright © Novello & Co., Ltd. International CopyRights Secured. All Rights Reserved. Reprinted by Permission of G. Schirmer, Inc. (ASCAP). **A-7:** "Hej pada pada"(Dewdrops) Slovak lyrics and music by Marie Winn and Alan Miller from The Fireside Book of Children's Songs, published by Simon & Schuster, copyright 1966, renewed 1994. Reprinted by permission. **A-8:** "¡Que gusto!" (What Pleasure!) English words by Ruth DeCesare. © Alfred Publishing Co., Inc. Used with permission of the publisher. **A-12:** "Hashkediya" (Tu b'Shvat Is Here) Music by M. Ravina, words by Y. Dushman, translation by S. Dinin, arranged by Harry Coopersmith from The Songs We Sing selected and edited by Harry Coopersmith, published 1950 by the United Synagogue Commission on Jewish Education. **A-13:** "Vamos a la mar" (Let's Go to the Sea) reprinted by permission of the Organization of American States. **A-14:** "La paloma blanca" (The White Dove) from Songs of Hispanic Americans, Selected, Edited and Arranged by Ruth De Cesare, Ph.D. An Educator's Resource Book of Folk Songs from the Mexican-American Border, the American Southwest and Puerto Rico, © 1991 by Alfred Publishing Co., Inc. **A-15:** "Inkpataya" Lakota courting song, by J. Bryan Burton. Courtesy World Music Press. **A-18:** "Karangatia ra" © 2002 Pearson Education, Inc. **A-19:** "Sarika keo"(Bird Song) Folk Song from Cambodia. Courtesy World Music Press. **A-27:** "Ah, eu entrei na roda" (I Came to Try This Game) Brazilian Singing Game from Games Children Sing Around the World. Edited by Paul Ramsier, Ph.D. © 2001 Warner Bros. Publications. All Rights Reserved. Used by Permission. WARNER BROS. PUBLICATIONS U.S. Inc., Miami, FL 33014. **A-29:** "Greetings" from My Harvest Home, 1995. Courtesy World Music Press. **A-33:** "El mes de abril," (The Month of April) from Cantemos en España, Vol. 1, by Beatrice and Max Krone. © 1936 Neil A. Kjos Music Co., San Diego, California. International Copyright Secured. All Rights Reserved. Used by permission 2003. **A-33:** "Hama chi dori" (Plovers) from 101 Favorite Songs Taught in Japanese School, translated by Ichiro Nakano. Used by permission of The Japan Times, Ltd. **A-35:** "Don Gato" © 1988 Silver Burdett Ginn. **A-39:** "El Rabel" (The Violin) from Songs of Latin America: From the Field to the Classroom adapted by Patricia Shehan Campbell with Ana Lucía Frega, p. 42. WARNER BROS. PUBLICATIONS U.S. INC. Miami, FL. 33014. **A-41:** "Hanuka, Hanuka" Words and music by Flory Jagoda from The Flory Jagoda Songbook: Memories of Sarajevo. Used by permission of Flory Jagoda. **A-48:** "Ichi-gatsu tsuitachi" (A New Year's Greeting) Words by Senge Takatomi, Music by Ue Sanemichi (Ichi-gatsu Tsuitachi) from The Magic of Music, © 1966 Ginn & Company. **D-13:** "The Juniper Tree" Copyright 1937 by John A. Lomax. Reprinted by permission of Global Jukebox Publishing. **E-2:** "Alligator Pie" from Dinosaur Dinner (With A Slice Of Alligator Pie) by Dennis Lee, © 1997 by Alfred A. Knopf, Inc. Rhythmic setting © 2002 Pearson Education, Inc. **E-3:** "Ding, Dong, Diggidiggidong" from Music for Children, Vol. 1, by Carl Orff and Gunild Keetman, © 1958 by Schott & Co. Ltd. London. **E-5:** "Ida Red" from 150 American Folk Songs to Sing Read and Play, © Copyright 1974 by Boosey & Hawkes, Inc. **E-6:** "Black Snake" **E-7:** "Mister Ram Goat-O" from Brown Girl in The Ring by Alan Lomax, J.D. Elder and Bess Lomax Hawes. Copyright © 1997 by Alan Lomax and Pantheon Books, a division of Random House, Inc. **E-9:** "Hosisipa" from Sing It Yourself by Louise Bradford. © 1978 Alfred Publishing Company. **E-10:** "Chicken on the Fence Post" from A Book of Nonsense Songs by Norman Cazdon. **E-15:** "The Juniper Tree" Copyright 1937 by John A. Lomax. Reprinted by permission of Global Jukebox Publishing. **E-17:** "Hop Up, My Ladies" Collected, adapted and arranged by John A. Lomax and Alan Lomax. TRO © Copyright 1941 (Renewed) Ludlow Music, Inc., New York, NY. **E-18:** "Don't Let Your Watch Run Down" from South Texas Work Songs by Gates Thomas, found in Publications of the Texas Folklore Society No. V, 1926, titled Rainbow in the Morning. **E-20:** "Don't Let the Wind" from The Kodaly Context by Lois Choksy. © 1981 by Prentice-Hall, Inc., Upper Saddle River, NJ. **E-23:** "Hashkediya" (Tu b'Shvat Is Here) Music by M. Ravina, words by Y. Dushman, translation by S. Dinin, arranged by Harry Coopersmith from The Songs We Sing selected and edited by Harry Coopersmith, published 1950 by the United Synagogue Commission on Jewish Education. **E-24:** "Pretty Saro" © 1940, 1964 Jean Ritchie Geordie Music Publishing Co. **F-2:** "I Don't Care If The Rain Comes Down" Traditional Folk Song. ORFF accompaniment © 2002 Pearson Education, Inc. **F-3:** "Oh, Won't You Sit Down" African American Spiritual. ORFF accompaniment © 2002 Pearson Education, Inc. **F-5:** "One Morning Soon" African American Spiritual. ORFF accompaniment © 2002 Pearson Education, Inc. **F-6:** "Old Texas" Cowboy Song from Oklahoma. ORFF accompaniment © 2002 Pearson Education, Inc. **F-7:** "Love Somebody" Folk Song from the United States. ORFF accompaniment © 2002 Pearson Education, Inc. **F-9:** "Alabama Gal" Folk Song from Alabama. ORFF accompaniment © 2002 Pearson Education, Inc. **F-10:** "Old Man Mosie" Singing Game from the United States. ORFF accompaniment © 2002 Pearson Education, Inc. **F-12:** "Tender Shepherd" (Count Your Sheep) from Peter Pan. Words by Carolyn Leigh, music by Mark Charlap. WARNER BROS. PUBLICATIONS U.S. INC., Miami, FL 33014 and Hal Leonard Corporation. ORFF accompaniment by Pearson Education, Inc. **F-13:** "The Groundhog Blues" from Music Play 25 Fun Lessons for Pre-K through 2nd Grade Classes by Gayle Giese. © 1997 Belwin-Mills Publishing Corp. WARNER BROS. PUBLICATIONS U.S. INC., Miami, FL 33014. **F-14:** "Li'l Liza Jane" Dance Song from the United States. ORFF accompaniment © 2002 Pearson Education, Inc. **F-16:** "Hop Up, My Ladies" Collected, adapted and arranged by John A. Lomax and Alan Lomax. TRO © Copyright 1941 (Renewed) Ludlow Music, Inc., New York, NY. ORFF accompaniment by Pearson Education, Inc. **F-19:** "Hush, Hush" African American Spiritual. ORFF accompaniment © 2002 Pearson Education, Inc. **F-21:** "Don't Let Your Watch Run Down" from South Texas Work Songs by Gates Thomas, found in Publications of the Texas Folklore Society No. V, 1926, titled Rainbow in the Morning. ORFF accompaniment by Pearson Education, Inc. **F-23:** "Now Let Me Fly" © 1995 Silver Burdett Ginn. ORFF accompaniment © 2002 Pearson Education, Inc. **F-25:** "Don't Let the Wind" from The Kodaly Context by Lois Choksy. © 1981 by Prentice-Hall, Inc., Upper Saddle River, NJ. ORFF accompaniment by Pearson Education, Inc. **F-27:** "Erdö, erdö de magos" (In the Silent Forest) Folk Song from Hungary. ORFF accompaniment © 2002 Pearson Education, Inc. **F-28:** "Turn the Glasses Over" Folk Song from the United States. ORFF accompaniment © 2002 Pearson Education, Inc. **F-30:** "Hashkediya" (Tu b'Shvat Is Here) Music by M. Ravina, words by Y. Dushman, from The Songs We Sing selected and edited by Harry Coopersmith, published 1950 by the United Synagogue Commission on Jewish Education. ORFF accompaniment by Pearson Education, Inc. **F-31:** "A Ram Sam Sam" Folk Song from Morocco. ORFF accompaniment © 2002 Pearson Education, Inc. **F-33:** "Pretty Saro" © 1940, 1964 Jean Ritchie Geordie Music Publishing Co. ORFF accompaniment by Pearson Education, Inc. **F-34:** "Vamos a la mar" (Let's Go to the Sea) reprinted by permission of the Organization of American States. ORFF accompaniment by Pearson Education, Inc. **F-35:** "He's Got the Whole World in His Hands" African American Spiritual. ORFF accompaniment © 2002 Pearson Education, Inc. **F-36:** "La paloma blanca" (The White Dove) from Songs of Hispanic Americans, © 1991 by Alfred Publishing Co., Inc. P.O. Box 10003, 16380 Roscoe Blvd., Van Nuys, CA 91410-0003. ORFF accompaniment © 2005 Pearson Education, Inc. **F-38:** "El mes de abril," (The Month of April) from Cantemos en España, Vol. 1, by Beatrice and Max Krone. © 1936 Neil A. Kjos Music Co., San Diego, California. ORFF accompaniment by Pearson Education, Inc. **G-2:** "Name, Name, What's Your Name?" by Jim Solomon. **G-8:** "Black Snake" **G-18:** "Greetings" from My Harvest Home, 1995. Courtesy World Music Press. **G-19:** "El mes de abril," (The Month of April) from Cantemos en España, Vol. 1, by Beatrice and Max Krone. © 1936 Neil A. Kjos Music Co., San Diego, California. International Copyright Secured. All Rights Reserved. Used by permission 2003. **H-5:** "Name, Name, What's Your Name?" by Jim Solomon. KEYBOARD accompaniment by Pearson Education, Inc. **H-7:** "Gypsy in the Moonlight" (Folk Song from Trinidad), from Caribbean Voyage: Brown Girl In The Ring. Courtesy of the Alan Lomax Archives. KEYBOARD accompaniment by Pearson Education, Inc. **H-15:** "Coffee Grows on White Oak Trees" Folk Song from the United States. KEYBOARD accompaniment by Pearson Education, Inc. **H-17:** "Hot Cross Buns (Version 1)" Arrangement © 1991 Silver Burdett Ginn. KEYBOARD accompaniment © 2002 Pearson Education, Inc. **H-18:** "He's Got the Whole World in His Hands" African American Spiritual. KEYBOARD accompaniment © 2002 Pearson Education, Inc. **H-20:** "Nani wale na hala" (Lovely Hala Trees) Folk Song from Hawaii. KEYBOARD accompaniment © 2002 Pearson Education, Inc. **H-27:** "Knock No More" Words and Music by Elizabeth Gilpatrick. © 1996 Alfred Publishing Co., Inc. KEYBOARD accompaniment by Pearson Education, Inc. **I-2:** "Hello to All the Children of the World", from We Sing Around the World by Pamela Conn Beall and Susan Hagen Nipp, Price Stern & Sloan, Inc., a division of Penguin Putnam Inc. RECORDER accompaniment